Coach service to Rapid City - 1989 (photo by Rick Mills)

I watched a train pass by today
Groping slowly on its way
Like someone in the dark of night,
Proceeds in fear, because he might
Stray from a path he cannot see
And continues onward cautiously

There was a time when night or day
A passing train sped on its way,
And we who watched it in its flight
Admired its speed and sound and might,
And hoped that luck would come our way
And we could ride that train some day,

Can this slow train I see be me?
Was the fast one only memory?
Of golden days when youth was mine
I sped along and saw no sign
Of the rough track that lay behind
The goal in life I tried to climb.

Harry Putnam
September 1988

Prairie Steamer by Jon Crane

Bingo Grain Company - Okaton, 1990 (photo by Rick Mills)

Milwaukee crew at Milbank - 1954 (photo by Bill Mohr)
from left to right
Vincent "Pop" Schell - Coal Shed Foreman
Frank Darrington - Section Laborer
Lloyd Bagaus - Section Foreman
Ernie Hanson - Signal Maintainer

III

Reflection on "the Cowboy" at sunset - 1990 (photo by Rick Mills)

Railroading in the
Land of Infinite Variety

A History of South Dakota's Railroads

Printed in the U.S.A.
Published by Battle Creek Publishing Company, Hermosa, South Dakota
Graphic Presentation and Printing by Simpson's Creative Printers, Rapid City, South Dakota
Typesetting by Simpson's Creative Printers, Rapid City, South Dakota
Binding by Register-Lakota Printing Company, Chamberlain, South Dakota

ISBN #0-9615321-3-0
Library of Congress #90-81796
All photos by Rick W. Mills, or of the author's collection, unless otherwise noted.

ACKNOWLEDGEMENTS

The author would like to acknowledge and sincerely thank the following individuals, museums, groups, and friends for their contributions in the completion of this work. A project of this size is never easy, but the names listed have made it much more enjoyable and definitely easier.

Neil Bagaus, Milbank, SD
Black Hills Railway Society, Rapid City, SD
Charles Bohi, White River Junction, VT
Brown County Historical Society, Aberdeen, SD
Greg Bunce, Dakota Southern Railway, Chamberlain, SD
Chicago and North Western Transportation Co., Chicago, IL
Codington County Historical Society, Watertown, SD
Dakota, Minnesota and Eastern Railroad Corp., Brookings, SD
J.S. and Diane Dale, Rapid City, SD
Tracy and Diann Dobbs, Black Hawk, SD
Barb Downen, Rapid City, SD
Larry Dilts, Newcastle, WY
Jerome Drager, C&NW Transportation Co., Chadron, NE
Robert Eddy, Chadron, NE
Mike and Lana Edwards, Rapid City, SD
John Ellison, C&NW Transportation Co., Rapid City, SD
James Ehernberger, Cheyenne, WY
Steven Friezen, Brookings, SD
Les Foran, Dakota, Minnesota and Eastern Railroad Corporation, Pierre, SD
Alex Huff, Dakota Southern Railway, Chamberlain, SD
Jeff Hendricks, Hettinger, ND
Don Jurrens, C&NW Transportation Co., Hermosa, SD
Gary Jurrens, Burlington Northern Railroad, Hermosa, SD
Clarence Kimball, Rapid City, SD
Wayne Kling, Burlington Northern Railroad, Gillette, WY
Joan Lintz, Hermosa, SD
R.C. Lathrop, Burlington Northern Railroad, Aberdeen, SD

Robert Larson, Sioux Falls, SD
Robert Larson, Rapid City, SD
Mike Mancuso, Sioux Falls, SD
J. Richard Mead, Rapid City, SD
Dr. David B. Miller, Black Hills State University, Spearfish, SD
Larry and Victoria Mills, Hermosa, SD
Wayne and Arlene Mills, Hermosa, SD
Doug Morgan, C&NW Transportation Co., Chicago, IL
Northern Hills Railway Society, Deadwood, SD
Robert P. Olmsted, Woodridge, IL
Chuck Park, Sioux Falls, SD
Harry Putnam, Rapid City, SD
Chris Randall, SD Department of Transportation-Division of Railroads, Pierre, SD
A.C. Roman, Rapid City, SD
Rapid City Public Library, Rapid City, SD
Kevin Ryan, Sioux Falls, SD
Daniel and Kathleen Simpson, Rapid City, SD
Johny Severson, Black Hawk, SD
South Dakota State Historical Society, Pierre, SD
David Strain, Rapid City, SD
Don Sours, Rapid City, SD
Ted Schepf, Elgin, IL
Leonard Tripp, Sioux Falls, SD
Greg and Linda Walters, Rapid City, SD
Western History Department, Denver Public Library, Denver, CO
A.J. Wolff, Cheyenne, WY

Table of Contents

Milwaukee F's on a westbound time freight at Milbank, SD in 1954. (Bill Mohr photo, Neil Bagaus collection)

- Dedication -

To the pioneers of Dakota;
the settlers, and the railroaders

Milwaukee Road section shed at Interior, SD - 1980
by David B. Miller

"Trains do something to me, make me sad, wondering forever at the earth again. We hurtle on in the darkness, down the never-ending road." - General George Patton

Foreword

The preceding quote by General Patton seems to be shared by a great number of people in one sense or another. It also appears that as a railroad is divided into specific geographic areas, it takes on a new character as well. People that I have interviewed and corresponded with in this project have conveyed their feelings regarding the perceived changes the railroads had as they entered the State of South Dakota, and the railroads do become something unique here.

Case in point. Railroad enthusiasts and historians acknowl-

edge the vital roles that the railroads played in the development of the High Plains. They also recall the vast number of problems and abandonments that have occurred in the area. Many do not realize the number of railroad lines that remain exist at all, or that the railroads that currently operate in South Dakota are the evolved entities of at least twenty-three predecessor lines that pioneered rails in the state. It is a great study, in many facets, of South Dakota's development as the railroads' history evolves after 1861, the year that President Abraham Lincoln created Dakota Territory. The story not only becomes one of the territorial, and later state, influences over the railroads, but the great powers of the railroads in creating the state we know today.

My part in this history? I have been fascinated by the railroad from my earliest memories. Unfortunately, those memories are of diesels, not the steam locomotives that had provided the power on the Black Hills Division of the Chicago and North Western about a decade before my birth. I often inquired of my parents, my grandparents, and various great aunts and uncles of those days when the railroads, and the romantic steamers, provided many of the necessities of everyday life. Their recollections gave me a great sense of history and pride in that icon we revere today as "the pioneering spirit of Dakota." I researched and found a decendant actually was a part of the crew to push the first rails of the Fremont, Elkhorn and Missouri Valley/Chicago and North Western through to Rapid City, Dakota Territory, and others to follow and settle near the line in 1889. Yes, they settled the year of statehood. Others came around the turn of the century to find their dreams in the newly opened areas of western South Dakota along the Milwaukee and North Western. And the story is repeated for many other residents of South Dakota.

This book represents approximately fifteen years of collecting information, recollections, and photos of the railroads in South Dakota on my part. There are others that have helped me a great deal; that almost goes without saying. While the majority of them are listed in the acknowledgements section, special recognition must be given to a couple of individuals. First, a great deal of appreciation is extended to Leonard Tripp of Sioux Falls. His faithful collection of railroad material over a period of decades has proved quite invaluable. I also would like to thank R.C. Lathrop of Aberdeen for his generous photo contributions to the effort.

To all of the readers of this work, my hopes that it recalls fond memories of that era that has passed and a greater appreciation of the railroads in South Dakota, past and present. My best wishes.

Rick W. Mills
January 1990

Chapter One

The Selling of Dakota

By the early fall of 1804, the Lewis and Clark Expedition had journeyed from St. Louis up to the center of the recently-acquired Louisiana Purchase. As they reached the villages of the various Indian tribes along the Missouri River, they heard stories of the vast lands they had, or were about to cover on their trek westward to find the great western ocean as directed by President Jefferson. They could only speculate as to what they would find, let alone what would happen to this region of the middle Missouri in the decades to come. Back in the eastern United States of America, the form of transportation that would be the dominant force of the rapid development in the new west was just coming of age.

Small railroads began to develop throughout the east beginning in the 1820's. They gradually expanded westward as their potential for both passenger and freight traffic was realized. Common carriers such as the Baltimore and Ohio began to replace certain toll roads and canals as the method for settlers to head for the new lands west of the Appalachians. Settlers moved in ever-increasing numbers across the middle part of the nation as new lands were opened for homesteading and mining. The California gold rush and subsequent boom in that new state caused the government to look at the possibility of a transcontinental railroad to link the two coasts.

Many of the new states and territories west of the Mississippi saw the lucrative aspects of such a line running through their property. Numerous routes were discussed and surveyed through the 1850's and up until other matters threw the nation into the Civil War. At the time of the outbreak of war, President Buchanan signed the document that created Dakota Territory.

The year was 1861. Dakota Territory had just been created as the Civil War laid siege to the country. The northern-controlled Congress then sought to route the railroad to the Pacific Ocean in a central location. President Abraham Lincoln signed

It would be another seven years before the fledgling territorial capital of Yankton, Dakota Territory would see a railroad in this 1866 view. Even as the capital started life as a "river town", the arrival of the Dakota Southern brought a rather quick end to the era of the steamboat on the "Big Muddy". (South Dakota State Historical Society)

the Pacific Rail Act into law on July 1, 1862 and set the stage for the first railroad to be built into the Dakota Territory. While not to enter the future state of South Dakota proper, the Union Pacific Railroad would have a profound influence on the history of the state's railroads up through to the present day. The southeastern part of today's state of Wyoming became home to a part of the transcontinental Union Pacific/Central Pacific Railroad. Cheyenne, Dakota Territory welcomed the advancing Union Pacific on November 14, 1867. The following was written by an inspired reporter for the Cheyenne Leader that day...

"Our citizens swarmed along the grade, and watched with the most intense delight and enthusiasm, the magic work of track-laying. The hearty greeting we all gave this gigantic enterprise, so rapidly approaching, was too deep and full for expression. There was no shouting and cheering, but one full tide of joy that sprung from the deep and heartfelt appreciation of the grandeur of the occasion and the enterprise, and that bright new future now dawning on the remote regions of the far west."

Prior to the completion of the Union Pacific in 1869, the Dakota Territorial Legislature was busy with the business of granting charters to would-be lines that were basing all or parts of their fortune on the Pacific Railroad. The first to be granted was issued in 1862 to the Missouri and Niobrara Valley Railroad Company, although it would be a decade before a line would actually be built in the future state of South Dakota.

The first trackage was built by the Winona and St. Peter Railroad, a subsidiary of the Chicago and North Western Railway, from New Ulm, Minnesota to Gary. Later that year, the first train rolled into the southeastern corner of the territory from Sioux City, Iowa to Vermillion. The Dakota Southern Railway to Vermillion had fought to enter the area ever since the legislature approved their charter back in 1867. In 1873, the two lines were extended farther into Dakota. While the North Western's St. Peter extended as far as Lake Kampeska, the Dakota Southern completed the first line into the territorial capital of Yankton. These first rail lines brought about a dramatic influx of immigrants from all over the country as well as from foreign lands. The wave of immigrants slowed as did the construction of new railroad lines due to the Panic of 1873. The panic did little to slow the tide of people coming to "south" Dakota the following years due to the Black Hills Gold Rush of 1874.

The "Magic Mountains" or Black Hills had been virtually at the center of the Sioux Indian culture for centuries. They were fabled to be the home to the "Great Manitou" of the Sioux, and therefore off-limits to humans. Rumors of the existence of gold had circulated before, but were finally acted on after an August, 1873 report by a scout from Fort Abraham Lincoln, Dakota. Indications

The Dakota Southern's first locomotive to operate into Dakota Territory was the American class 4-4-0 named Judge Brookings. That first line into the southeasternmost part of the territory was not the first line into Dakota (the Winona and St. Peter subsidiary of the Chicago and North Western reached Gary in 1872 as did the DS into Vermillion), but signalled the beginning of the Great Dakota Boom that was to follow the rails as they progressed across the state. (Courtesy of Leonard Tripp)

Another of the Dakota Southern's early locomotives is shown in this view at Yankton in 1874. The locomotive "Black Hills" was apparently named by the railroad to show what the line's ultimate ambitions were after that year's gold discovery across the territory. (South Dakota State Historical Society)

were that a sizeable amount was located on the western slopes of the Hills. The government had been grappling with the Panic for nearly a year, and the benefits of such a strike seemed to outweigh the treaties already set with the Sioux regarding their sacred "PAHA SAPA". On the government's order, a group of 1,200 cavalrymen led by General George A. Custer journeyed to the Black Hills to confirm the presence of gold. That they did. Near the present city of Custer, the supposedly well-kept secret became front page news across the country in just over a month. The year of 1874 put the area of the Black Hills of "south" Dakota on the lips of the nation. The Panic of 1873 really did not abate until the middle of 1877, however, the influx of would-be millionaires and soon-to-be farmers launched Dakota toward the recovery and boom years from 1879 through to 1885.

The railroads rebounded and began again to push across the territory in 1878. The area around Sioux Falls became the focal point in the first years of the boom, and was reached by the first train of the Worthington and Sioux Falls Railroad on August 1, 1878. This predecessor of the Chicago, St. Paul, Minneapolis and Omaha Railroad (a subsidiary of the Chicago and North Western) was extended on into Salem the following year. In 1879, the predecessor of the Chicago, Milwaukee and St. Paul reached Sioux Falls as well. The Sioux City and Pembina and the first rail line to Yankton, the Dakota Southern, were consolidated and officially absorbed into the Milwaukee system the following year. Also in 1879, the first stretch of mining railroad was built by the Homestake Mining Company in the Black Hills at Lead. The tiny steamer was freighted across the western prairies from Bismarck on the Missouri River. A section of line was built as far as Volga in 1879 as well by the Dakota Central Railway. The following year that line would become a primary link in the race between the Chicago and North

Headlines across the country in the summer of 1874 did little to discourage goldseekers headed to the Black Hills of Dakota.

As the prospectors headed to the Black Hills, the railroads of Dakota began to promote passage to as close to the area as possible via their lines. The Northern Pacific ended up in the state to the north, but in the early 1880's the railroad was doing its part.

VOL. III. NO. 156.   CHICAGO, FRIDAY MORNING, AUGUST 28 1874.

THE GOLD FEVER.

Intense Excitement in the City Yesterday Over the News from the Black Hills.

The Mining Offices and Bullion Dealers Invaded by Anxious Inquirers.

General Sheridan Warns Miners and Prospectors to Keep Away from the Scene.

As by Treaty that Section is Exempt from Settlement by the Whites.

Some Doubts as to Whether All the Gold Region is Within the Reservation.

THE BLACK HILLS COUNTRY.

DISTANCES.

From Chicago to Bismarck, 1,000 miles.
From Bismarck to Black Hills, by the route followed by General Custer, 490 miles.
From Brule City to Harney's Peak about 155 miles, the proposed route being along the valley of the W
From Harney's Peak to Fort Laramie, 150 miles.
The dotted line represents the route pursued by Custer's command to Harney's Peak. He returns by road.

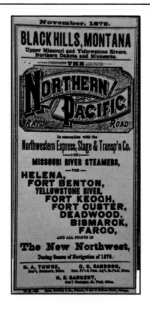

Western and the Chicago, Milwaukee and St. Paul for dominance in eastern Dakota.

North Western President Marvin Hughitt conducted a personal survey of the Dakota prairies and concluded that if a railroad were built out to the Missouri River, and possibly beyond to the gold fields in the Black Hills, it would eventually draw settlers to the lands around it. The subsidiary Dakota Central sought to do just that, and in the spring and summer pushed westward from Volga to the Big Muddy at East Ft. Pierre, later shortened to Pierre. Well, if the North Western could do it, then Milwaukee President Alexander Mitchell thought it could be done better by his line. The Milwaukee pushed across roughly fifty miles to the south of the Dakota Central/North Western to terminate at the new Missouri River town of Chamberlain, named for a director of the railroad. The Milwaukee also started a line across from Ortonville, Minnesota to Webster which would eventually become a part of the Milwaukee's transcontinental extension through to Seattle. Dakota Central constructed a line up from just west of Brookings on the Pierre main to connect with the Winona and St. Peter line (another North Western subsidiary) at Watertown. The general northward trend continued in 1881.

Aberdeen became the center of railroad activity in 1881 with three lines completed into town that year. The longest line to Aberdeen was built through from the Milwaukee president's namesake city of Mitchell in competition on the northern end with the Dakota Central's Huron to Aberdeen trackage. With the Milwaukee holding a slight edge in the traffic going to the southeastern corner and to Sioux City, the Dakota Central built southeasterly from Iroquois to the North Western at Hawarden, Iowa in 1882. As the lines began to resemble the stitches of a crazy quilt, the initial carrier line was established in the isolated Black Hills. The Black Hills and Ft. Pierre completed fifteen miles of line out from

Bull and oxen teams were utilized across the prairies and across the lands west of the Missouri River to freight goods before the rails arrived - Rapid City, Dakota in 1885. (Courtesy of Eva Streeter)

The tent and shanty town of Deadwood, Dakota shortly after the discovery of gold in the gulch in 1875.

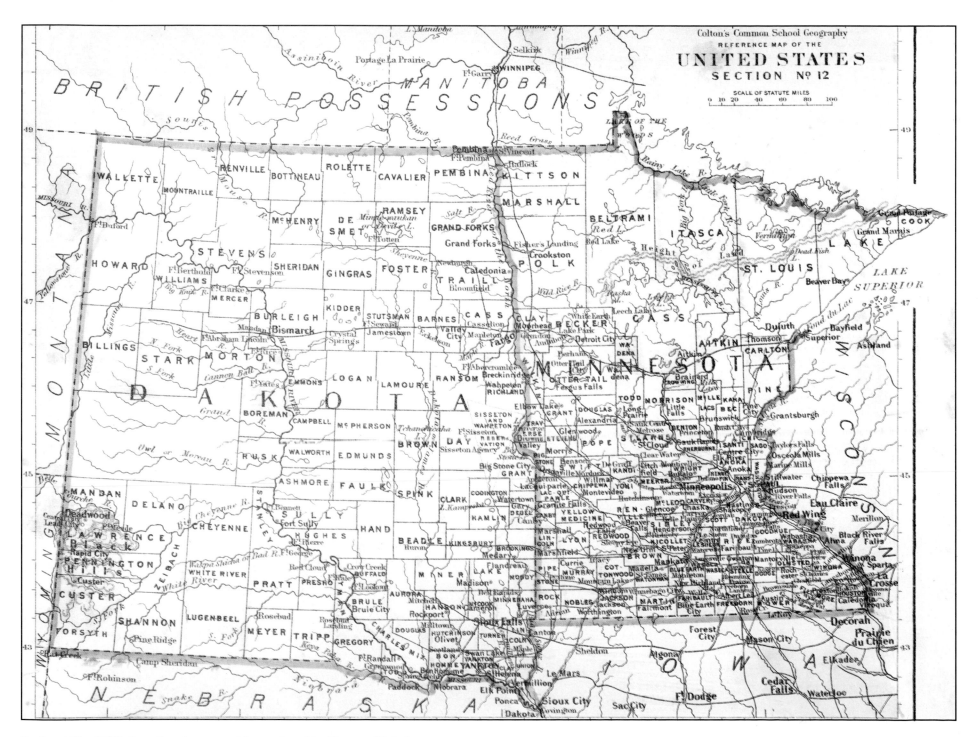

By the middle of 1880, the railroads were reaching westward in all areas of Dakota.

A Sioux City and Pacific 4-4-0 is posed at Valentine, Nebraska in 1883. The Sioux City and Pacific engine was operating on the Fremont, Elkhorn and Missouri Valley Railroad, the SC&P's subsidiary, just a year before both were leased by the Chicago and North Western. The North Western then extended the Elkhorn line toward the booming Black Hills.

Lead to Bucks Landing to the primary region of timber for the rapidly expanding Homestake Gold Mine. But some of the hearty souls of the mining camps were also treated to picnic excursions and basic transportation in the early days of operation.

While the North Western/Milwaukee competition continued in the eastern part of the state, several new railroads were beginning to make inroads. In 1884, the Minneapolis and St. Louis and the Burlington, Cedar Rapids and Northern reached Watertown. The solicitation for the masses of immigrants coming to Dakota was nearly as fierce as the railroad construction itself. A large percentage of the settlers in the 1879 to 1885 era were native-born Americans, but overseas immigrants made up a minority of the railroad's efforts. All of the railroads issued various flyers, booklets, and handouts to extoll the virtues of the Dakota lands along their respective right-of-ways. A Milwaukee pamphlet of 1885 "quotes" a farmer in Faulk County...

"My advice to every man without a home is, come to Dakota and get one."

The towns, the farms, and the railroads were booming by the end of 1885. Hundreds of new towns were served by the various branches of the North Western and Milwaukee systems in the eastern part of southern Dakota. West of the Missouri, freighters with oxen and bull teams drug the supplies of survival overland to the gold cities of the Black Hills. Out in the very southwestern part of the territory, a railroad was advancing toward a settlement called Buffalo Gap.

A Chicago, Milwaukee and St. Paul train arrives at Fedora, Dakota with immigrants ready to homestead in the new lands of Dakota.

The railroads were to face many blizzards after this photo of a Winona and St. Peter(C&NW) train fighting the drifts on the line from Minnesota to the Pierre in 1881. The North Western's goal to push this line to the Black Hills would not be realized for almost another three decades. (South Dakota State Historical Society)

A short Dakota Central(C&NW) train rolls west across the James River trestle at Huron, Dakota Territory in the 1880's. The North Western and the Milwaukee competition in the state would continue from the earliest days up into the first decades of the twentieth century. (South Dakota State Historical Society)

As the railroads promoted settlement along their respective lines, they distributed photographs of the sights along the right-of-way. The Chicago and North Western commissioned several photographers to show the masses the farms and other successful endeavors in Dakota. The following six views of the eastern part of the state on the main line from Huron to Brookings are typical of the efforts of the various railroads to promote the territory. (Courtesy of the Chicago & North Western Transportation Company)

04591 BROOKINGS, S.D. HARVESTING ON THE CALDWELL FARM

04552 HURON, S.D. A VALLEY FARM

BROOKINGS, S.D. HARVESTING ON THE OLESON FARM.

Heading for the Hills

With the confirmation of gold in the Black Hills, it was only a matter of time before the Sioux would be pushed out and the settlers and miners would push their way in. At the beginning of the rush in 1875 and 1876, the closest railroad to the Hills was the Union Pacific nearly 200 miles to the south. Over 300 miles separated the gold fields from the Northern Pacific on the north, and about the same distance from the Dakota Southern to the east at Yankton. In the eleven years prior to the arrival of a standard gauge railroad after the gold disclosure, various stage lines and private freighting companies delivered goods, passengers, and the mail to the Black Hills mining camps. The first documented run was by the Spotted Tail Express and Stage Company of Cheyenne up to Custer City on March 8, 1875. Various other lines ran into the area from the Missouri River towns and the railheads on the Union Pacific at Sidney, Nebraska and Cheyenne; Bismarck and Mandan on the Northern Pacific, and the Dakota Southern and Missouri River at Yankton and Fort Pierre.

The earliest citizens of the area felt that they would greatly benefit from having a railroad that connected them with the eastern part of the territory. It would simply be an improvement to be connected by rail to anywhere. The first rails to be laid in the Black Hills were in 1879, as the Homestake Gold Company began its great expansion underground. The first engine on the line, the J.B. Haggin, was transported from Bismarck to Lead by oxen team that summer. The Homestake blossomed, and set about building the first actual common carrier narrow-gauge railroad in 1881. Grandly named the Black Hills and Fort Pierre Railroad, the railroad was built primarily for the use of Homestake's timber operations southeast of Lead, but reflected the desire to connect with an outside line. (The Dakota Central/North Western reached Pierre that same year.) Year by year, the BH&FtP crept toward the eastern edge of the Hills, hoping to

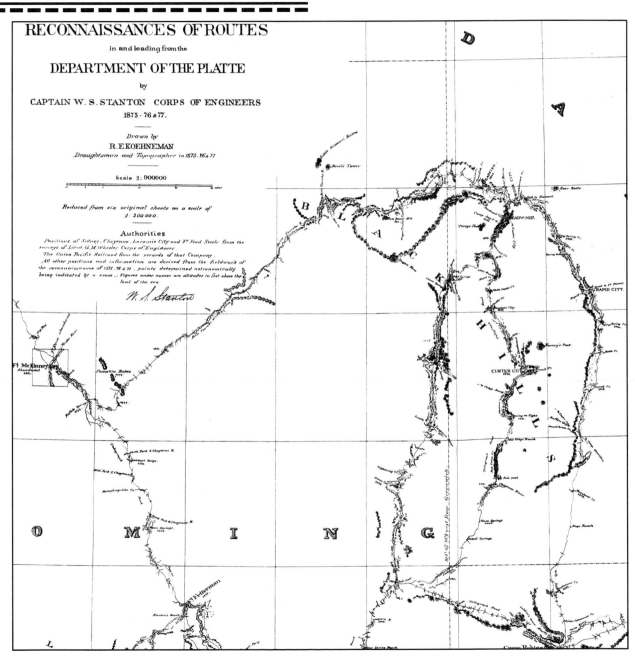

The Black Hills as mapped out in 1877 by the Army Corps of Engineers (courtesy of J.S.Dale)

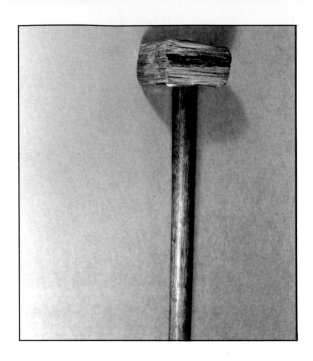

Above: When the Elkhorn was completed to Buffalo Gap, a group of Custer City businessmen brought a mica hammer to pound the last spike home. The hammer is preserved today at the Minnesela Museum in Rapid City.

Top Right: Buffalo Gap, Dakota in 1886

Opposite: The Elkhorn agent has hung out the sign, and this FE&MV box car has become the first depot at Rapid City, Dakota in this photo taken on July 4, 1886. The location would soon see the first frame depot constructed to serve the future "Gateway to the Black Hills". The freight house to the right is near the corner of Maple and East St. Joseph street in today's Rapid City.

eventually connect up with a railroad from the east. Help was on its way.

The Fremont, Elkhorn and Missouri Valley Railroad(the Elkhorn) had been taking its time in moving northwesterly out of Fremont, Nebraska after it was created in 1869. It had just what the Black Hills wanted, an outlet for passengers and goods via the Union Pacific connection at Fremont. Also, the line connected with the Chicago and North Western Railroad east of Fremont at Missouri Valley, Iowa. The construction of the Elkhorn in northern Nebraska had progressed to Valentine in 1883. By this time, the North Western had benefitted from the misfortunes of Elkhorn management, and leased the line. With additional capital, the Elkhorn/ North Western team was ready and in good position to "Head for the Hills", something the North Western was not able to do from its eastern Dakota lines. The Great Sioux Reservation from the Missouri to east of the Black Hills was off-limits to the men and their iron horses. With the northern Nebraska route of the Elkhorn, the North Western could continue west and swing northward along the eastern slopes of the Black Hills range and legally gain access to the booming Black Hills. That they did, and finally ran a train into the first Black Hills railhead of Buffalo Gap, Dakota on November 28, 1885.

The following year, the rails were completed into Rapid City and the first train arrived to great fanfare on July 5,1886. A symbolic race was held between the Sidney-Deadwood Stage in which the train arrived slightly ahead of the coach at the Rapid City station. The Elkhorn was also the star attraction as it rolled the first standard gauge passenger train into Deadwood on November 29,1890. The North Western's Elkhorn had won a symbolic victory here as well, as the first train of the North Western's Black Hills competition lost by nearly a month.

The advancing Chicago, Burlington and Quincy Railroad and its subsidiaries Burlington and Missouri River/Grand Island and Wyoming Central, were a force in the development of the southern and central regions of Nebraska. By the fall of 1889, the Grand Island and Wyoming Central was inside the southwestern corner of the newly proclaimed state of South Dakota. With eyes on the coal deposits of Wyoming Territory and the mining

Rail laid by the Black Hills & Fort Pierre Railway in 1882 still carried a few cars on the North Lead line for the Burlington Northern in late 1982.

Black Hills & Fort Pierre 2-6-0 was the last locomotive built by Baldwin Locomotive Works for the line.It was renumbered 533 when the CB&Q bought the railroad in 1904. (Courtesy of William Eley)

towns of the Black Hills, the GI&WC founded the town of Edgemont as a base camp and junction of the two lines. The spring of 1890 found crews busy putting a line through the center of the Hills to compete with the Elkhorn on the eastern edge. Elkhorn and North Western forces resisted a Burlington entrance into Deadwood, but in the end held it off only long enough to beat them by a month. In the Burlington's quest to reach Deadwood, they found themselves taking over the two independent narrow gauge railroads that existed prior to the standard gauge lines arrival.

The aforementioned Black Hills and Fort Pierre and the smaller Deadwood Central Railroad were taken over in 1901 and 1893 respectively. The Deadwood Central was formed by local interests in 1888 to serve as a commuter line between Deadwood and Lead. They also acquired a right-of-way up to the Black Hills and Fort Pierre line near Englewood. That line was utilized by the GI&WC/Burlington by simply leasing the line and installing a third rail to standard-gauge the narrow gauge line. The combined system under the Burlington gave them additional competitive trackage that served most of the areas that the Elkhorn's narrow gauge lines served above Deadwood and Lead in the Ruby Basin Mining District. It was generally believed that the Burlington's consumption of the two independent narrow gauge lines was an attempt to keep the Elkhorn's 1891 narrow gauge trackage construction from eventually linking up with the established lines and possible takeover by the FE&MV/North Western.

As the Grand Island & Wyoming Central subsidiary of the Burlington & Missouri River Railroad, a subsidiary of the Chicago, Burlington & Quincy(Burlington) built north through the heart of the Black Hills, specialized steam shovels were called on to do the chores. This view of a Julian shovel is between Pringle and Custer in the summer of 1890.

While the Burlington and North Western faced off in the mining areas, they also built other feeder lines to other parts of the Hills. The Burlington sent a spur through the scenic Spearfish Canyon to the city of Spearfish. The Elkhorn headed north from the Deadwood line at Whitewood to the Belle Fourche River valley where the city of Belle Fourche was established. Belle became an important cattle and sheep center and many thousands of carloads originated here for the railroad. Many of the livestock headed southeast to the slaughterhouses of Omaha, Sioux City, Chicago, and Sioux Falls.

Back at Sioux Falls, several new railroads had entered the eastern South Dakota railroad scene by statehood in 1889. The increasing agricultural and mining shipments from the territory had prompted the St. Paul, Minneapolis and Manitoba Railroad to build several lines into the state. Watertown was reached by James J. Hill's Manitoba, and later Great Northern, in 1887. The next year saw the line from Watertown extended to Huron by the Manitoba subsidiary Duluth, Watertown and Pacific. Also in 1888, the Manitoba reached the thriving center of Sioux Falls via subsidiary Willmar and Sioux Falls. The year of statehood saw a future Great Northern line reaching Aberdeen from Rutland, North Dakota. In addition to the Great Northern trackage built in that decade, the North Western and Milwaukee continued to build feeder lines to new towns in the center of South Dakota. Two more lines reached to Sioux Falls in the 1880's as well; the Dubuque and Sioux City (predecessor of the Illinois Central) and a branch of the Burlington, Cedar Rapids and Northern that already served Watertown. All of the three new lines, and the Milwaukee and the North Western, were having pangs of transcontinental fever.

Jim Hill was already proceeding across North Dakota and westward toward the coast, but he was looking at least at the possibility of a southwestern route to Denver. Lines from Huron and from Yankton (which extended from Sioux Falls in 1893) were surveyed that would have headed near or slightly south of the Black Hills. The Chicago, Rock Island and Pacific (the Rock Island) controlled the Burlington, Cedar Rapids and Northern as well as the Minneapolis and St. Louis lines at this time.

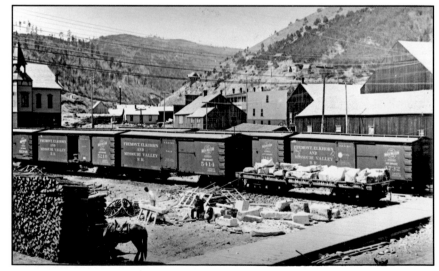

Following the surveyors, the graders, the blasters, and the shovels were the track crews. In this classic view near the present site of the Crazy Horse Memorial north of Custer, the crews pose with their equipment for the lens.

Stone quarried for the new Elkhorn depot in Deadwood is yet to be unloaded in this view in the early 1890's. The gulch in the back center of the photo continues on to Central City. The Elkhorn three-rail was routed up the gulch as far as Central, where it became a single narrow gauge track to the Ruby Basin Mining District. (Centennial Archives, Deadwood Public Library)

19

They were conducting surveys of their own at the time from around Watertown to the west and northwest as far as San Francisco and western Canada. The Illinois Central subsidiary Midland Pacific was created to build a transcontinental line through to the Black Hills and on into Wyoming, Idaho, and to the area of Portland, Oregon. There was still an obstacle west of the Missouri however. The railroads retained their lobbyists in Washington trying to clear a path through that pesky Indian Reservation out toward the Black Hills. Through political moves and loss of Indian lives, the reservation was cut through to allow transportation and settlement of parts of the "West River country" of South Dakota.

The Black Hills were finally about to see a railroad from the eastern part of the state. Their mines were still producing ample quantities of precious metals as well as timber. Livestock beyond compare were being shipped out in record numbers on the Chicago and North Western. Both it and the Burlington chose to consolidate all of the various West River and Black Hills subsidiaries in the first several years of the twentieth century. But it was not the Burlington that would challenge North Western for the last area of South Dakota's settlement, that honor would be saved for the Milwaukee.

The completed FE&MV depot in Deadwood, 1895. (R.C. Lathrop collection)

The Burlington and Missouri River depot at Deadwood that was shared with the narrow-gauge Deadwood Central Railroad. A DC train in from Lead is pictured in the lower right. (Centennial Archives, Deadwood Public Library)

With the Elkhorn depot nearly eight blocks east of downtown Rapid City, a horse drawn streetcar was installed to transport passengers. The tracks ran directly west up Main Street, and terminated near today's Hilton Hotel at Eighth and Main.

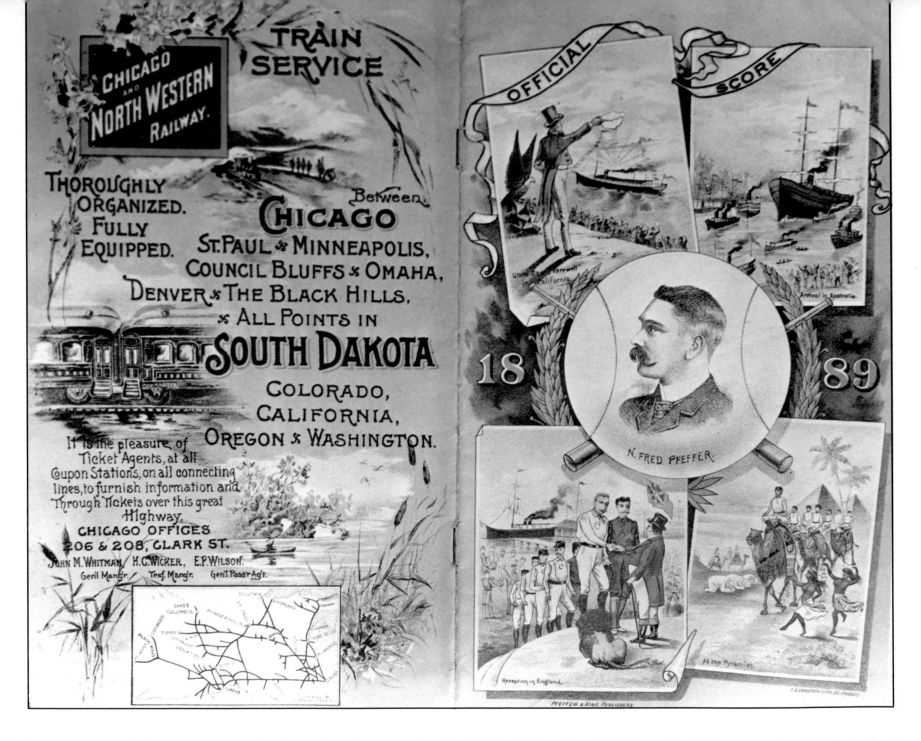

On the back cover of an 1889 baseball program sponsored by the Chicago and North Western Railroad, the Black Hills in the newly-established state of South Dakota are touted up in fine fashion. (courtesy of the Chicago & North Western Transportation Co.)

With all of the big boys promoting around them, the Black Hills & Fort Pierre and the Deadwood Central got together in the early 1890's to do some "PR". The DC train is pictured at their siding at the east side of Lead, while the BH&FP sits alongside their depot on the northwest side of town. The two narrow gauge lines would survive for about a decade before becoming another spoke in the Burlington wheel.

23

Elkhorn class G 4-8-0s #208 and #209 are at the fledgling mining camp of Terry in 1892. The Elkhorn completed just over 18 miles of lines into the mining districts above Central City and Lead, most within a stone throw of the Burlington's BH&FP and DC lines.

A polished Sioux City & Pacific 4-4-0 poses at the Hot Springs station in the middle 1890's. The SC&P originally controlled the Elkhorn until its owner, John Blair, fell upon hard times and leased the two lines to the North Western in 1884. (courtesy of the Chicago and North Western Transportation Co.)

The Burlington and Missouri River contributed quite a number of American class 4-4-0s to the Burlington's fleet when merged in 1904. One of these that did honors in Nebraska, Wyoming, and in South Dakota basks in Denver after its relettering and renumbering. Ironically, this Rhode Island Locomotive Works graduate came to the B&MR in 1889.

The North Western publicity shooters were not only busy in the eastern part of the state, but also in the Black Hills. This view from the White Rocks area above Deadwood shows the upper area of the city, with the rival Burlington's freight house and yard parallel to the street at the center. (courtesy of the Chicago and North Western Transportation Co.)

In the southern Black Hills, the warm springs near Hot Springs were the prime attraction. Elkhorn/ North Western trains ran into the city via a 14 mile spur from the main at Buffalo Gap, passing near this spot. (courtesy of Chicago and North Western Transportation Co.)

Other vistas of the Black Hills were promoted in North Western advertising than those immediately adjacent to their lines. These photos of tourists enjoying boating and scenic tours near Sylvan Lake were made in the mid 1890's. (courtesy of Chicago and North Western Transportation Co.)

THE COACH TO SYLVAN LAKE. S.D.

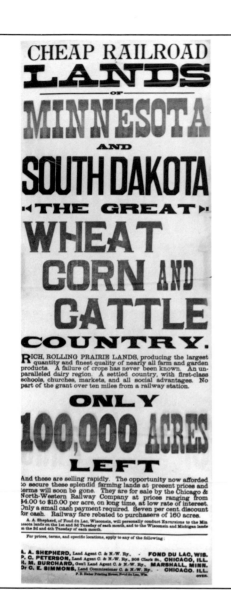

With Brookings as the site of the state Land Grant College, the North Western promoted it as a part of its agricultural package. This view looks south from the SD State University campus to Brookings. (courtesy of Chicago and North Western Transportation Co.)

To promote the progressive spirit of the state, a photo of the first Huron College quarters was included. (courtesy of Chicago and North Western Transportation Co.)

Illinois Central 4-4-0 #1115 heads for Sioux Falls on the Cherokee line. (Leanard Tripp Collection).

Before crossing the Big Sioux River, the Illinois Central erected a wooden depot at East Sioux Falls. (Leanard Tripp Collection).

In a view looking west, the stone depot of the Illinois Central dominates the foreground. The trestle over the Big Sioux belongs to the Milwaukee. (Leonard Tripp collection)

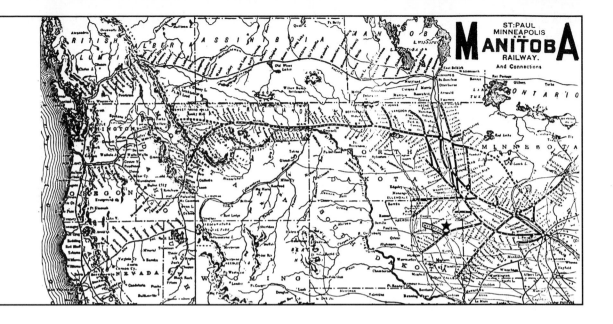

⁂THE⁂

ST. PAUL, MINNEAPOLIS & MANITOBA

RAILWAY

—IS THE—

···GREAT·THROUGH·LINE···

TO AND FROM

WATERTOWN. SOUTH DAKOTA.

An early 1890's photo of the Great Northern depot, water tank, and a passenger train at Sioux Falls. After the rails were completed into Sioux by the Great Northern's predecessor St. Paul, Minneapolis and Manitoba on November 1, 1889, the line to Yankton was surveyed and finished in 1893. (Leonard Tripp collection)

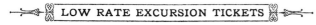
From early on, the Omaha was visibly controlled by the North Western. The station at Sioux Falls was no exception. (Leonard Tripp collection)

As an American class 4-4-0 stops to take on water at Valley Springs, the fireman prepares to fill the tender. Note the Omaha Road initials under the cab window. (Leonard Tripp collection)

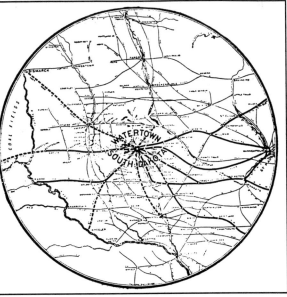

Railroad Facilities.

WATERTOWN is pre-eminently the railroad center of South Dakota; no other city in the State has so many actual avenues of entrance by railroad, or the prospect of so large and important addition to her present rail facilities in the near future. Watertown now has seven operated lines of railway (exclusive of the Watertown and Lake Kampeska), the survey for another has been finished—upon which work will soon commence—and two more lines are projected by organized companies with fair prospects of being completed before the close of next year. Watertown's railroad facilities, as may be seen from a hasty glance at the accompanying map, place our manufacturers, jobbers and merchants in communication with the rest of the world, under exceedingly favorable circumstances. No other inland city in the Northwest offers such superior advantages for freights, while the volume of traffic, rapidly

This ingenious little train ran between Watertown and the resort of Lake Kampeska in the 1890's. (SD State Historical Society)

Pride in the job is evident in this photo of an Omaha engine crew at Valley Springs. Note the lanterns for use by the head-end brakeman. (Leonard Tripp collection)

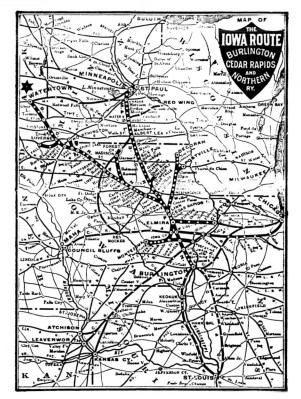

Upon arrival at Sioux Falls, in 1886, the BCR&N constructed a magnificent two-story station. The BCR&N controlled the Minneapolis and St. Louis Railroad until shortly after the turn of the century, about the same time the Rock Island absorbed the "Iowa Route". (Leonard Tripp collection)

A classic pose by a BCR&N 4-4-2 Atlantic class illustrates the road's pride in its power. Atlantics were primarily used for passenger service. (Leonard Tripp collection)

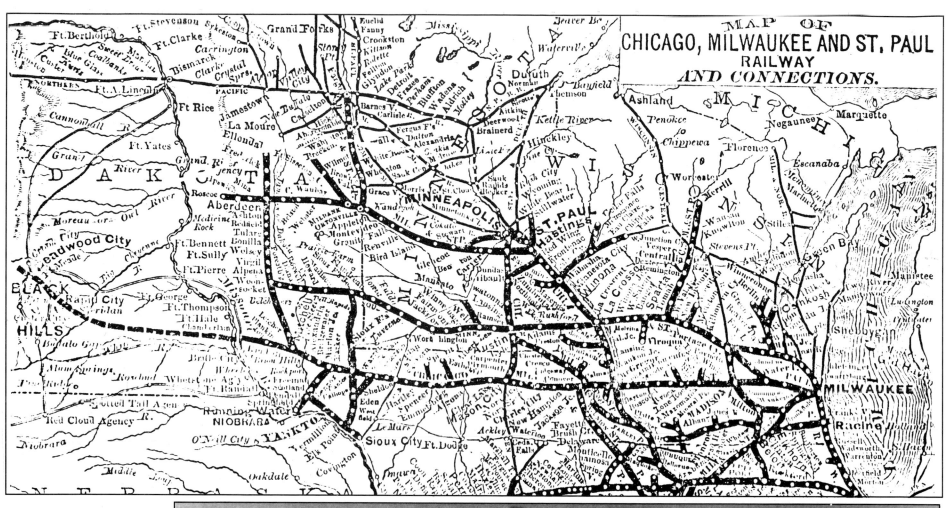

MAP OF
CHICAGO, MILWAUKEE AND ST. PAUL
RAILWAY
AND CONNECTIONS.

The CM&StP roundhouse at Aberdeen, circa 1895. (R.C. Lathrop collection)

As the Milwaukee planned its westward expansion at the turn of the century, a drawing of their plans was used in company booklets. Their visionary ideas were to bear some fruit in the next century.

A Chicago, Milwaukee and St. Paul 4-4-0 is dwarfed by its larger cars as it leads them eastbound out from Vermillion. This was a part of the first Dakota Southern line from Sioux City in 1872. (W.H. Over Museum Photo Archives, USD)

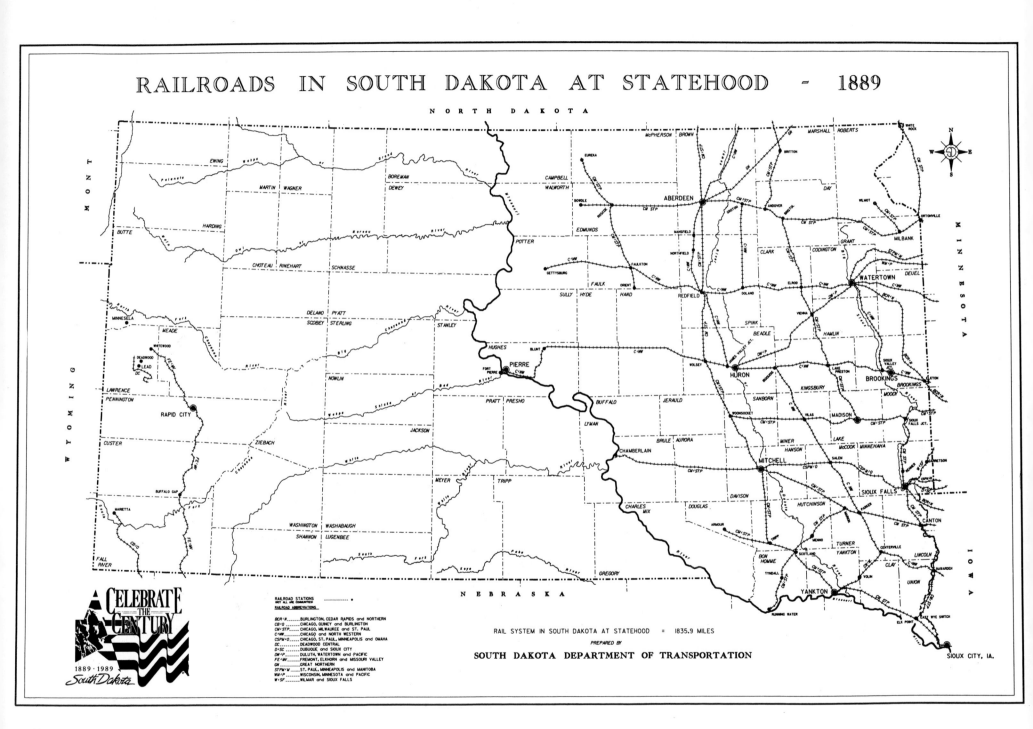

RAILROADS IN SOUTH DAKOTA AT STATEHOOD — 1889

NORTH DAKOTA

MONTANA

WYOMING

MINNESOTA

IOWA

NEBRASKA

RAILROAD STATIONS .... ●
(NOT ALL ARE COMMUNITIES)

RAILROAD ABBREVIATIONS

BCR·N .... BURLINGTON, CEDAR RAPIDS and NORTHERN
CB·Q .... CHICAGO, QUINCY and BURLINGTON
CM·STP .... CHICAGO, MILWAUKEE and ST. PAUL
C·NW .... CHICAGO and NORTH WESTERN
CSPM·O .... CHICAGO, ST. PAUL, MINNEAPOLIS and OMAHA
DC .... DEADWOOD CENTRAL
D·SC .... DUBUQUE and SIOUX CITY
DW·P .... DULUTH, WATERTOWN and PACIFIC
FE·MV .... FREMONT, ELKHORN and MISSOURI VALLEY
GN .... GREAT NORTHERN
STPM·M .... ST. PAUL, MINNEAPOLIS and MANITOBA
WM·P .... WISCONSIN, MINNEAPOLIS and PACIFIC
W·SF .... WILMAR and SIOUX FALLS

RAIL SYSTEM IN SOUTH DAKOTA AT STATEHOOD = 1835.9 MILES

PREPARED BY

SOUTH DAKOTA DEPARTMENT OF TRANSPORTATION

CELEBRATE THE CENTURY

1889·1989
South Dakota

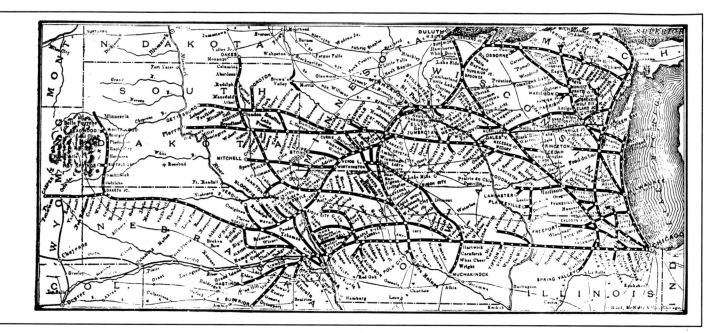

MAP OF THE CHICAGO & NORTHWESTERN

RAILWAY SYSTEM.

A feeder line for the Elkhorn was the Wyoming and Missouri River. The short line ran from Belle Fourche to Aladdin, Wyoming to tap several coal mines and cattle loading points. Locomotive #1, leased from the Elkhorn, is ready to take a cattle train to Belle in this photo.

Built in 1890, the Forest City and Sioux City Railroad reached only as far as Gettysburg. The line was supported by the C&NW over its 21 year existence, as in these views of leased C&NW 2-6-0s. It has been suggested that only one engine was leased to the FC&SC, but has not been confirmed. The primary revenue for the line was the transportation of goods to Forest City for the Cheyenne River Indian Agency across the Missouri River. A ferry provided transportation on the intermediate leg of the trip to freight wagons on the other side. The Forest City line became nearly obsolete after the Milwaukee crossed the river at Mobridge in 1907, and pushed a line down to the reservation in 1910. The FC&SC was abandoned in 1911. (SD State Historical Society)

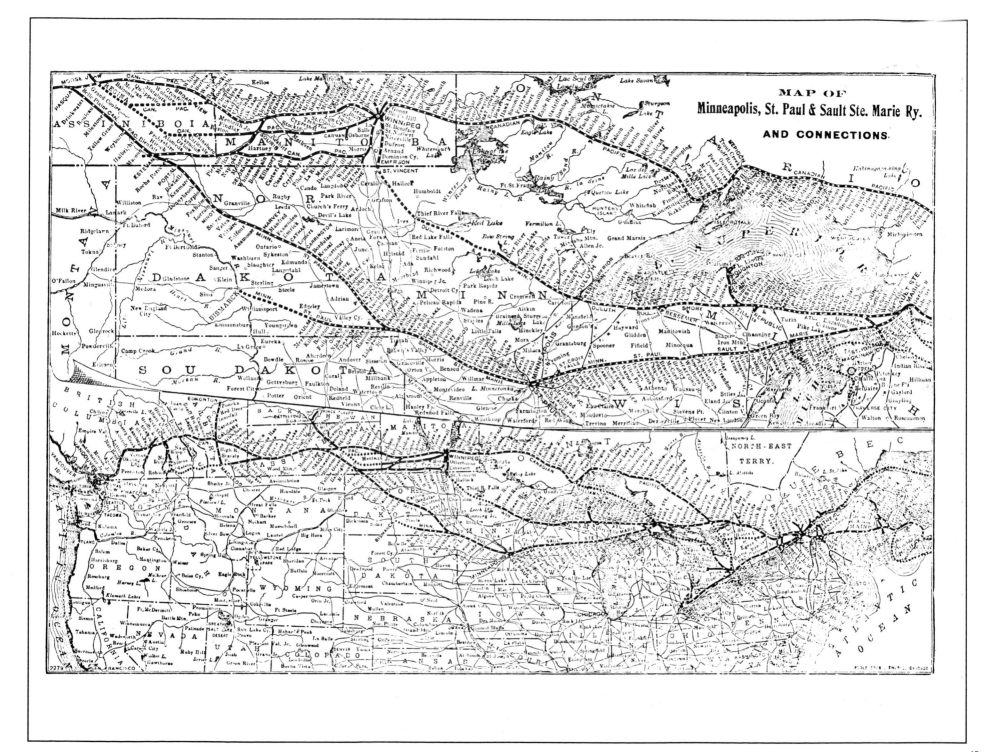

MAP OF
Minneapolis, St. Paul & Sault Ste. Marie Ry.
AND CONNECTIONS.

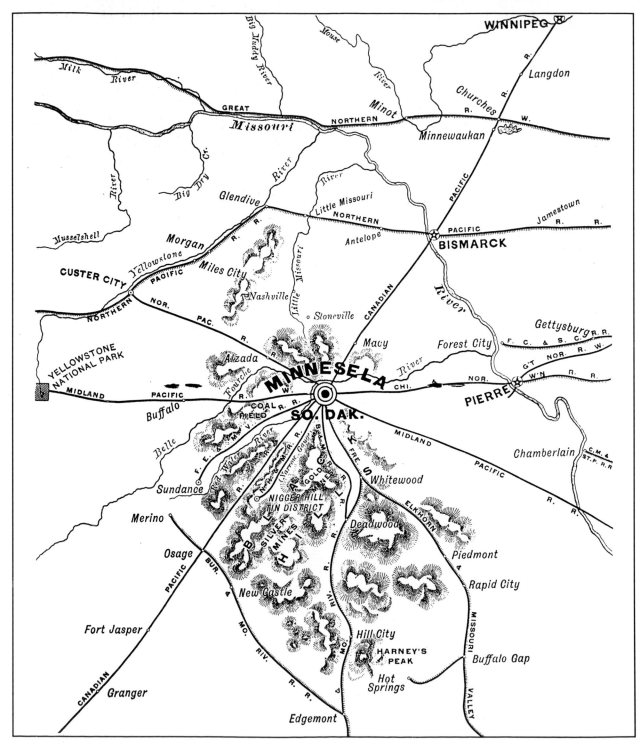

The town that lived by the paper railroads, and died by the lack of real ones was Minnesela, Butte County. This map distributed by the Minnesela boosters in 1890 was designed to promote a city that the Fremont, Elkhorn and Missouri Valley line from Rapid City was sure to terminate in. But an upstart called Belle Fourche that was several miles to the northwest received the Elkhorn line, and Minnesela became a ghost town.

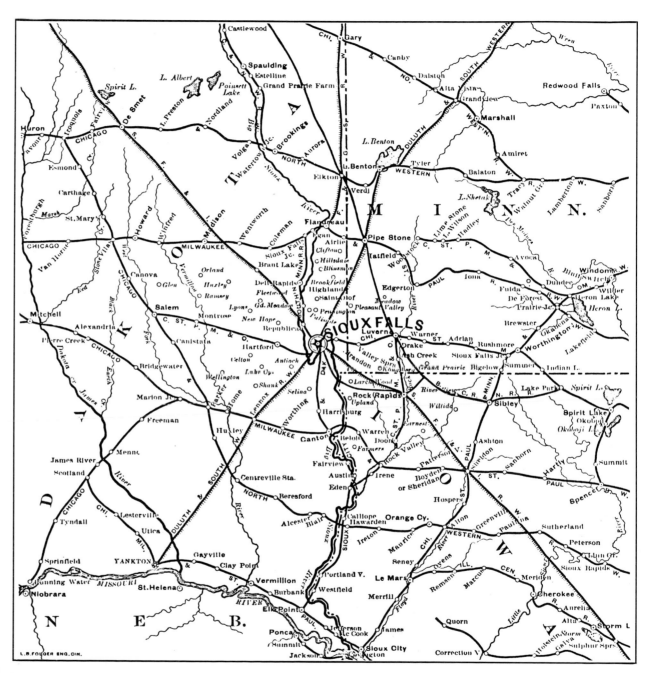

Another city that had its fortunes riding high on the rails was Sioux Falls. While most of these lines were completed, not all of the lines on the map materialized. (Leonard Tripp collection)

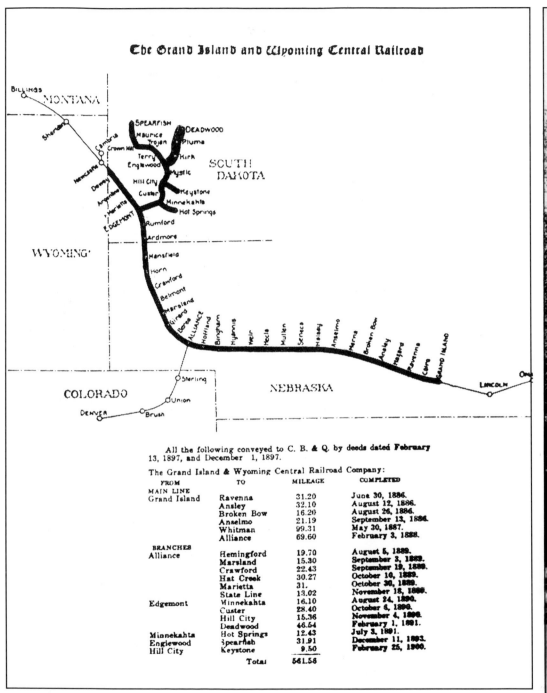

The Grand Island and Wyoming Central Railroad

On the Burlington's scenic branch line to Spearfish, the tracks followed Spearfish Creek down the Spearfish Canyon past Spearfish Falls. Spearfish was obviously used enough to describe this beautiful area.

A proud crew poses by their locomotive at the Burlington yards in Deadwood in the wild 1890's. The little B&MR 0-6-0 is resting alongside the Minneapolis Brewing Company plant just to the west of the freight station. (Centennial Archives, Deadwood Public Library)

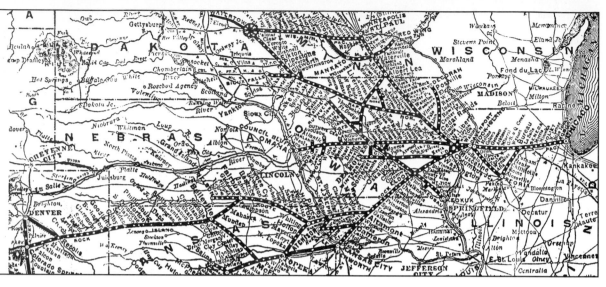

MINNEAPOLIS & ST. LOUIS RAILWAY,

"ALBERT LEA ROUTE,"

Between WATERTOWN. St. Paul, Minneapolis, Chicago. Council Bluffs. Kansas City and St. Louis.

As the Minneapolis and St. Louis Railroad pushed west from Watertown, they built a number of these practical stations. Conde became the junction of the "Louie `s" Missouri River line and the line to Aberdeen and Leola. (SD State Historical society)

48

In 1877, the Great Sioux Reservation had just been cut back to exclude the Black Hills. Compare that with a map from the middle 1890's, when the railroads and homesteaders had been granted two paths/land grants through to the Black Hills.(Rapid City Public Library)

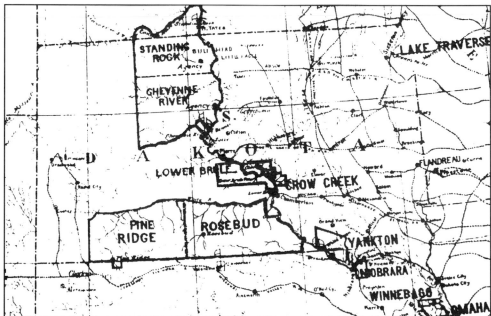

Pierre was poised to become the capital city in the late 1890's. This view of their rapid transit of the day, and one of their impressive hotels suggests a town ready for a challenge.

One of the North Western's classic high-stepping class C-6 4-4-0s is posed for the builder's camera at Schenectady Locomotive works in 1893. The North Western quickly changed over to 4-6-0s when they became available.

The Milwaukee continued to build feeder lines in the eastern part of the state up until the time of the great West River expansion after 1904. In this scene, a Milwaukee crew is laying down the line into Wessington Springs in 1903. (SD State Historical Society)

A southbound passenger is posed for the lens at the Horseshoe curve north of Custer. The Burlington and Missouri River Railroad, as well as its parent CB&Q, rostered a large number of the 4-6-0s as pictured above. (SD State Historical Society)

3625. "Harney Range."
shoe Curve on the B & M R'y near Custer
S. D.
and copyright '91 by Grabill P. & V. Co.,
and Hot Springs S. D.

An Elkhorn 4-6-0 is backing a passenger into Deadwood over the three-rail main from the yard. The line to Central City diverged just to the right of the photo, with the stub tracks branching off to several warehouses and the passenger station. The rails to the right above the locomotive are those of the Burlington and Missouri River spur to the Deadwood Smelter. (Centennial Archives, Deadwood Public Library)

The Black Hills and Fort Pierre not only fielded a number of narrow-gauge steamers, but had a pretty nice house for them. The BH&FP roundhouse in Lead offered six stalls plus a machine shed for the road's power. Compare the early view with the other view taken in 1984. Just imagine the Volkswagen is a 2-8-0.

Burlington 0-6-0 #1472 and its crew are posed at Edgemont in the early 1900's. The yard and roundhouse there made for an interesting junction of the main lines and the branch into the Hills.

Before the perfection of many of the standard safety devices on the railroad, accidents such as this occurred. With the advent of air brakes and more efficient cars and locomotives, wrecks decreased to an extent. The human factor still needed watching however.

Probably the most famous railroad photo in South Dakota is the classic "Three Trains at Lead." Shown in this are the narrow-gauge Deadwood Central passenger train at the bottom, the narrow gauge Fremont Elkhorn and Missouri Valley train behind locomotive #208, and a Homestake ore train at the top. Note the Homestake has also positioned one of their newest compressed air engines at the right side of their bridge.

Mr. V.T. Price, President,
Rapid City, Missouri River
& St. Paul Railroad Company

Dear Sir;—
The surveyed line of the Rapid City, Missouri River
and St. Paul Railroad started at Rapid City, South
Dakota, crossed the divide between Rapid Creek
and Box Elder Creek at a point three and one- half
miles from Rapid City, thence down Box Elder
Creek for a distance of 41 miles, thence down the
Cheyenne River for about five miles, thence up Bull
Creek 10 miles to the divide, thence down the fa-
mous "Bad River Valley" across the ceded Sioux
Indian Reservation 106 miles distant to the Missouri
River. The information you desired may be stated
thus;

Length of line from Rapid City to Pierre,...................165.55 miles
    maximum curvature, which occurs in all six
    times, - five times on Bull Creek and
    once on divide east of Rapid City,.....................6 degrees
Maximum grade, which occurs three times 1.5%
Total amount of earth work, (cu.yds.),.............................2,362,000
Total amount of loose rock work,(cu.yds.)..........................58,100
Grubbing and clearing, (Squares),..792
Bridging; -
    5 truss bridges (60 lin. ft. each),............................300 feet
    Amount of lumber required,......................2,908,000 B.M.
    Piling in entire line,...136,820 feet
    culvert pipe,..10,400 feet

Number of miles already graded,..16

Respectfully yours,

Myron Willoy
Chf. Eng.

Rapid City, Mch 15,1895.

During the campaigning to decide the site of state government in 1904, more than the cities and politicians of Pierre and Mitchell got into the act. A Milwaukee 4-4-0 is shown at a stop in Aberdeen as it promotes "its" candidate.

If the line described above sounds slightly familiar, it is because the engineers for the Chicago & North Western copied it as they began the final line to the Black Hills in 1905. Some of the most desolate and beautiful country in the state was about to be pioneered as the North Western and the Milwaukee set out from the Missouri River in a race across the ceded Sioux lands for Rapid City. This trans-state race was a direct result of the just completed Capitol contest between the Milwaukee's Mitchell and the ultimately successful Pierre, served by the North Western.

Since attaining statehood nearly a decade and a half before, the 1904 South Dakota State Legislature was still debating as to a permanent home for the state government. Pierre had held it the longest prior to then, and was ready to fight for it. On the other hand, Mitchell felt it was closer to the greatest centers of population in the east and southeast parts of the state. The Milwaukee wanted its Mitchell to have the title in the worst way. Special trains were run by the railroad to bring folks into town and give them a good time. The North Western did the same for Pierre, and according to South Dakota historian

Doane Robinson, "South Dakota simply suspended business and went out for a grand sixty day's picnic." The voters answered in the fall election with a yes for Pierre. The Milwaukee's candidate had lost, and almost immediately decided that it would spite the North Western by building west from Chamberlain to the Black Hills.

The North Western was put on the defensive. Sure, it had given land for the new State Capitol in Pierre as it had for the old structure, but would it answer the new challenge? President Marvin Hughitt quickly committed to a line from Pierre to Rapid City, and also pledged to beat the Milwaukee across. The great land opening between the Missouri and the Black Hills was on.

The Milwaukee pushed west from the Missouri to Murdo during 1906, while the North Western pushed from both ends - completing from Rapid City to Wasta, and from Pierre to Philip. The Milwaukee was also laying new rails to the north. The Chicago, Milwaukee and St. Paul Board of Directors had given their nod to an incredible plan to push the Milwaukee to the Pacific coast of Washington. So, the year of 1906 found Milwaukee rails at MO. BRIDGE. Mobridge, the name that would stick for their terminal and the new town on the river.

In 1907, the North Western completed its line

The Milwaukee's first bridge over the Missouri at Chamberlain in 1905. The fickle Missouri was once described by the editor of the Sioux City Journal; "Of all the variable things in creation, the most uncertain are the action of a jury, the state of a woman's mind, and the condition of the Missouri River." His dangerous editorial was echoed by the editor of the Presho newspaper that claimed "Every time a shower comes up, the Chamberlain bridge goes out."

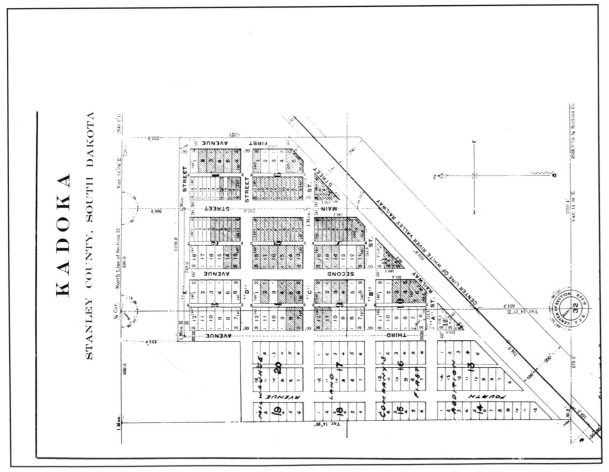

KADOKA
STANLEY COUNTY, SOUTH DAKOTA

As plattted out next to the Milwaukee's construction subsidiary White River Valley Railway, a 1907 projection of Kadoka. (Leonard Tripp collection)

to Rapid City in early July, while the Milwaukee made it into Rapid about a month later. Rapid City then began its climb as the supply and retail center of the western part of the state. The new lands west of the river became one of the last great land rushes in the country after the arrival of the new rail links. Both of the railroads boasted/advertised their new West River lines as the "Last, Best West." The land was branded as the last chance to get a cheap, productive piece of ground in the west. The scene in towns along the soon to be opened lands in October, 1907 was almost beyond belief. In the registration town of Presho, prospective farmers and ranchers came on as many as six trains a day, by wagon, on horseback and on foot, and by a few of the new contraptions called automobiles to take a chance on one of the homesteads in the million-acre tract. At one point in the registration, over 25,000 people waited in Chamberlain because there were not enough trains and crews on the Milwaukee to get them over to Presho. The events were much the same down on the North Western's new branch up from Norfolk, Nebraska through Gregory and Dallas to Winner. At Dallas, one group in from Chicago numbered 3,000 alone. The land itself was not free to the winners in the drawings, as it cost an average of $1,000.00 per 160 acre claim. Many of the losers in the early land lottery moved on to seek their fortunes in the Black Hills or on further west.

On May 14, 1909, the last spike in the Chicago, Milwaukee and St. Paul's transcontinental main line to Tacoma, Washington was driven at Garrison, Montana. Through freight service was initiated on July 4, 1909, and local passenger service the next day. West of Mobridge, the railroad was operated by the Milwaukee subsidiary Chicago, Milwaukee and Puget Sound. A branch line was completed from Moreau Junction to Trail City in 1910, where it

The locals come out to watch as the rails are spiked down on the Pierre, Rapid City & North Western Railway in 1907. The PRC&NW owned ten class Q 4-6-0s which later became C&NW numbers 497-506.

A scene of the surveyor's camp on Bull Creek near Wall. A 1.5% grade was eventually located in this area to get the line out of the Cheyenne River valley to the tablelands to the east.

split to send lines to Faith and to Isabel. The line gave the railroad access to the Standing Rock and Cheyenne River Indian Reservations, and to the expanding agricultural areas of the north central part of the state. Whether or not the Milwaukee should have built the transcontinental line is still debated today, as it was at the time of its construction and completion. The lands of the Pacific Northwest apparently reached their peak production around 1910, and the Canal was opened to commercial vessels in 1914. Couple those facts with the competition from the Hill lines(Great Northern and Northern Pacific) and the Union Pacific, and an ominous picture began to develop for the Milwaukee at an early date regarding the Pacific extension.

The rapid expansion of the railroads in the century's first decade was not limited to the West River country however. The fledgling South Dakota Central Railway pushed a line up from Sioux Falls to Watertown over a three-year period that ended in 1907. The line was reorganized after getting into financial trouble in 1916, and was renamed the Watertown and Sioux Falls. The Great Northern took an interest in the line that connected two cities it already served, and promptly took over the line within that year.

Another line still looking to be a part of the western expansion was the Minneapolis and St. Louis. They pushed a new line out to the Missouri River settlement of LeBeau in 1907, beginning at the town of Conde. President Edwin Hawley envi-

FIRST TRAIN INTO DEADWOOD FROM CAPITOL. CONDUCTOR. WILLIS SCHENCK. DEADWOOD, S. D.

Celebration time in Deadwood on July, 14, 1907 as the first North Western train from Pierre arrives. Also in the center of the photo is a narrow gauge train in from Central City and the Ruby Basin.

The first Milwaukee train from Chamberlain and Murdo to Rapid City passes through the Badlands near Scenic on July 20, 1907.

sioned his road to the Pacific, or at least to a connection with one of the Canadian transcons, much like his predecessors during the Louie's time in the Rock Island camp in the 1880's and 1890's. He also had a line pushed northwest from Conde to Leola, passing through Aberdeen in the process. Part of the line northwest from Aberdeen had actually been planned out in the 1890's as a branch of the Minneapolis, St. Paul and Sault St. Marie (Soo Line) from Bismarck. It was widely considered that the Leola extension might eventually join up with the then developing Midland Continental in North Dakota. The Midland was envisioned by its directors as the first north-south line from Canada to the Gulf Coast. It was built little by little, but never reached out of south-central North Dakota. With Hawley's untimely death in 1912, the short-lived "Empire Builder" era came to an abrupt end on the M&StL.

From the first years of the twentieth century until about 1920, the railroads were at their collective zenith in the state. Railroad building had come to a virtual end by the time of the First World War, with a wide variety of railroads in operation. From the busy main line of the Milwaukee on the north, to the thriving branches of the Soo Line, Great Northern, the M&StL, Illinois Central, Rock Island, the Omaha, the North Western, and the Milwaukee, plus the maze of lines in the Black Hills; it was a fascinating time. But it not only seemed too good to be true, it was.

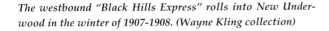

The westbound "Black Hills Express" rolls into New Underwood in the winter of 1907-1908. (Wayne Kling collection)

The sharp-dressed PRC&NW agent poses with the mail cart at the Nowlin depot shortly after the line's completion. The North Western operated this office into the early 1940's. (R.C. Lathrop collection)

New Station, Okato...
By J.M.Hamilton, Highla...

Magic City—
Murdo S.D. Apr.8/08.
By J.M.H.

Prosperity on the plains in these three views on the Milwaukee's Black Hills Division west of Chamberlain. The new line created the towns of Okaton, the "Magic" City of Murdo, and Draper - complete with an example of the other new form of transportation. (R.C Lathrop collection)

DRAPER

#21 DEPOT DRAPER, S.D.

C.C.BLACK & CO
SIOO FALLS, S.D.

An eastbound Minnesota Express is pausing at the new Pierre station in the teens. Note the Missouri River bridge spans in the center left of the photo.

The fury of the elements, especially flooding in the Black Hills area, played havoc with the railroads. This view in the spring of 1907 in Dark Canyon west of Rapid City on the Rapid City, Black Hills and Western (the Crouch Line) is a testimonial to that. (courtesy of Mary Farrar)

A slightly different view of the three railroads in Lead in this 1907 view. Differences in equipment are evident on all lines as well, with an electric CB&Q trolley in the foreground, a standard-gauge C&NW steamer in the middle right, and a compressed air locomotive handling the Homestake chores on the top track.

South Dakota Central 4-4-0 #1. (Leonard Tripp collection)

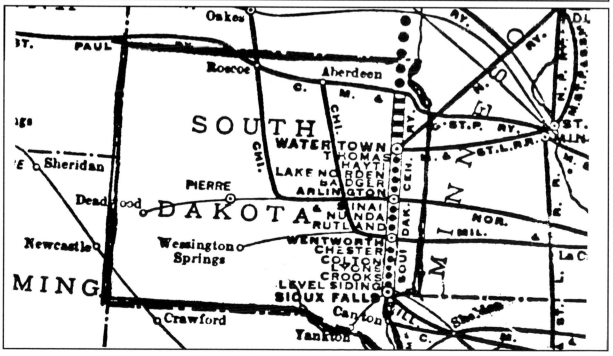

SDC #1 is captured on film as it pulls the first train into Wentworth on October 27, 1905. (Leonard Tripp collection)

A double-header heads out to clear the SDC main to Watertown. (Leonard Tripp collection)

Great Northern #3038 rests at Willmar, Minnesota around 1910. The GN's branch to Watertown split off from the main line to Sioux Falls here, with the main continuing on to the northeast at the Twin Cities. (Leonard Tripp collection)

Great Northern's gas-electric motorcar ready for departure from Sioux Falls at Watertown in the teens. (Leonard Tripp collection)

As the Omaha Road became more controlled by the C&NW, more North Western equipment was used into Sioux Falls and Mitchell. Here a C&NW 4-4-0 rests at Valley Springs. (Leonard Tripp collection)

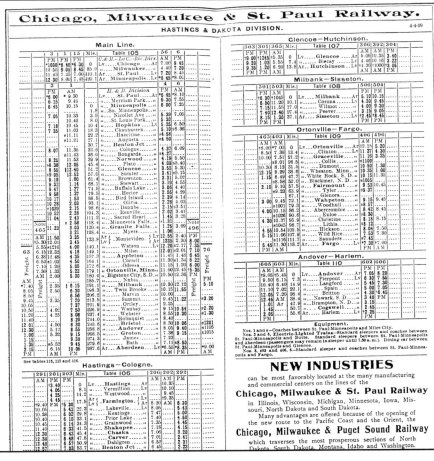

Main Line. — Table 105

Stations (Main Line): Chicago, Milwaukee, St. Paul, Minneapolis (U. & M.—La C.—Ric. Divs.)

H. & D. Division: Merriam Park, Minneapolis, So. Minneapolis, Nicollet Ave., St. Louis Park, Hopkins, Chanhassen, Hazeltine, Augusta, Benton Jct., Cologne, Bongards, Norwood, Plato, Glencoe, Brownton, Stewart, Buffalo Lake, Hector, Bird Island, Olivia, Danube, Renville, Sacred Heart, Minnesota Falls, Granite Falls, Myers, Montevideo, Watson, Milan, Appleton, Correll, Odessa, Ortonville Minn., Bigstone City S. D., Nubia, Millbank, Twin Brooks, Marvin, Summit, Ortley, Wahby, Webster, Holmquist, Bristol, Andover, Groton, James, Bath, Aberdeen

See tables 113, 115 and 116.

Hastings—Cologne. — Table 106

Stations: Hastings, Vermillion, Westwood, Farmington, Lakeville, Keatings, Prior Lake, Grainwood, Shakopee, Chaska, Carver, Dahlgren, Benton Jct.

Glencoe—Hutchinson. — Table 107

Stations: Glencoe, Biscay, Hutchinson

Milbank—Sisseton. — Table 108

Stations: Milbank, Corona, Wilmot, Peever, Sisseton

Ortonville—Fargo. — Table 109

Stations: Ortonville, Clinton, Graceville, Collis, Dumont, Wheaton Minn., White Rock S. D., Blackmer N. D., Fairmount, Tyler, Glenora, Wahpeton, Woodhull, Abercrombie, Enloe, Christine, Lithia, Hickson, Wild Rice, Saunders, Fargo

Andover—Harlem. — Table 110

Stations: Andover, Pierpont, Langford, Spain, Britton, Newark S. D., Brampton S. D., Cogswell, Harlem

Nos. 1 and 4—Coaches between St. Paul-Minneapolis and Miles City. Nos. 3 and 6, Electric-Lighted Trains—Standard sleepers and coaches between St. Paul-Minneapolis and Butte. Standard sleepers between St. Paul-Minneapolis and Aberdeen (passenger may remain in sleeper until 7.30 a. m.). Dining car between St. Paul-Minneapolis and Glencoe. Nos. 3, 403 and 406, 6—Standard sleeper and coaches between St. Paul-Minneapolis and Fargo.

NEW INDUSTRIES

can be most favorably located at the many manufacturing and commercial centers on the lines of the

Chicago, Milwaukee & St. Paul Railway

in Illinois, Wisconsin, Michigan, Minnesota, Iowa, Missouri, North Dakota and South Dakota.

Many advantages are offered because of the opening of the new route to the Pacific Coast and the Orient, the

Chicago, Milwaukee & Puget Sound Railway

which traverses the most prosperous sections of North Dakota, South Dakota, Montana, Idaho and Washington.

Chicago, Milwaukee & St. Paul Ry.
JAMES RIVER DIVISION.   4-4-09

Chicago—Aberdeen. — Table 111

Stations: Chicago, St. Paul, Mitchell, Aberdeen

Mitchell—Aberdeen—Edgeley. — Table 112

Stations: Mitchell, Loomis, Letcher, Cuthbert, Woonsocket, Alpena, Virgil, Wolsey, Bonilla, Spottswood, Tulare, Redfield, Ashton, Mellette, Duxbury, Warner, Aberdeen, Westport, Barnard, Frederick, Winship S. D., Ellendale N. D., Duane, Monango, Edgeley

Aberdeen—Mobridge—Linton. — Table 113

Stations: Aberdeen, Fife, Mina, Grady, Ipswich, Beebe, Roscoe, Gretna, Bowdle, Alamo, Java, Selby, Sitka, Glenham, Mobridge, Roscoe, Hosmer, Hillview, Eureka, Greenway S. D., Zeeland N. D., Hague, Strasburg, Linton

Nos. 1 and 4—Standard sleeper between Aberdeen and Marmarth. Coaches between St. Paul-Minneapolis and Miles City. Nos. 3 and 6, Electric-Lighted Trains—Standard sleepers and coaches between St. Paul and Minneapolis and Butte.

Roscoe—Orient. — Table 114

Stations: Roscoe, Loyalton

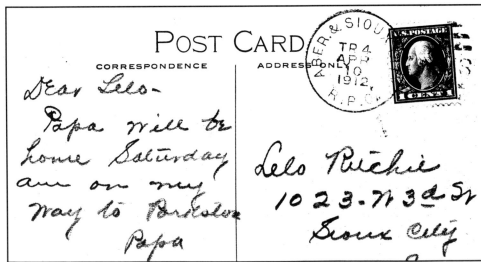

POST CARD

CORRESPONDENCE   ADDRESS ONLY

Postmark: ABER. & SIOUX ... TR 4 APR 10 1912 R. P. O.

U.S. POSTAGE 1 CENT

Dear Lelo—

Papa will be home Saturday am on my way to Portalon

Papa

Lelo Ritchie
1023 N 3d St
Sioux City

A violent flood raced through Deadwood on June 1, 1909 and damaged both railroads including the area around the North Western roundhouse. (Wayne Kling collection)

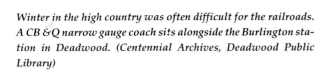

Winter in the high country was often difficult for the railroads. A CB &Q narrow gauge coach sits alongside the Burlington station in Deadwood. (Centennial Archives, Deadwood Public Library)

The Lands Registration Office in Presho was a busy place in this view in early October, 1907.

A North Western train arrives at the Gregory depot after the land bonanza of 1907.

The first passenger train to depart Winner rounds a curve eastbound out of town in 1911. (SD State Historical Society)

A Milwaukee steamer has just eased its train into the Rapid City depot, and the passengers are headed uptown. (courtesy of Mary Farrar)

Originally built in 1889 by the Cooke Locomotive Works as Iowa Central Railroad #61, Minneapolis and St. Louis B-1 0-6-0 #47 switches the yard at Watertown. (Codington County Historical Society, Watertown)

One of the North Western's spiffy Taunton Locomotive Works 4-4-0's poses with crew and train in Watertown. The #458 came to the railroad in 1881, and was scrapped in 1909. (Codington County Historical Society, Watertown)

Train time at the Great Northern station in Watertown, circa 1910. (Codington County Historical Society, Watertown)

A Great Northern passenger train has pulled into the stub-tracked GN station in Aberdeen. Note the GN freight house to the right of the train, and impressive Brown County Courthouse to the left. (Codington County Historical Society, Watertown)

This ornate depot at the end of the Milbank to Sisseton branch served the Milwaukee well; Sisseton, 1909. (SD Historical Society.)

The first Chicago, Milwaukee and St. Paul train arrives at Timber Lake on July 7, 1910. The branch would also be extended on into Isabel that year. (SD State Historical Society)

The Milwaukee's terminus at Faith in 1910. Note the two stall engine shed and the water car setting in front of it, as the water was rather tough to come by.

An immigrant train arrives in Faith shortly after the line's completion. The term dry-land farming was about to come into play.

A classic American class 4-4-0 of the Milwaukee arrives at Millard. The 4-4-0s were truly the engine that won the west and the frontiers of South Dakota. (R.C. Lathrop collection)

This burly 2-6-6-2 for the Chicago, Milwaukee and Puget Sound line west of Mobridge was captured on film in Aberdeen shortly after the engine was built in the teens. The steep grades through the Rockies of Montana and Idaho made locomotives like this feasible on the Milwaukee's transcontinental route to the Pacific.

During the construction of the Belle Fourche Irrigation Project and Orman Dam in the years around 1910, several small steamers were used to get the dirt moved. (courtesy of Wayne Kling)

The "famous" cannon balls from the Cannon Ball River territory on the Standing Rock Line of the Milwaukee are shown in Mobridge. (SD State Historical Society)

The Chicago and North Western's depot in Highmore, circa 1910. (Steve Friezen collection)

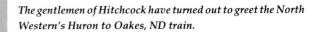

The gentlemen of Hitchcock have turned out to greet the North Western's Huron to Oakes, ND train.

Redfield was a busy point on the North Western for many years, as this scene in the teens attests to. The North Western ran lines into town from all four directions, and a great deal of passenger changeovers and interchange occurred at this simple structure.

Train time on the Minneapolis and St. Louis at Leola, north-west of Aberdeen.

The delivery cart is backed up to the platform at Delmont to receive goods in from the daily Milwaukee train from Yank-ton. (Leonard Tripp collection)

During the harvest season, lines of wagons like these on the Milwaukee at Faulkton delivered the crops to the elevators. Intense competition existed for the crops by not only the railroads, but between the elevators. (SD State Historical Society)

Busting the drifts on the North Western's Redfield to Blunt line in 1917. (Clarence Kimball collection)

"BOES" BEATING THEIR WAY TO N. DAKOTA ON A C. & N.W. FREIGHT TRAIN AUG. 13—1914

PHOTO B
HERSEY & HER
HECLA, S.

The "preferred" method of transient farm hands, or hoboes, is depicted in this view of a northbound C&NW train at Hecla. (SD State Historical Society)

The Milwaukee's presence in Aberdeen is obvious in this view. (SD State Historical Society)

Two views of the Omaha Road's section crews at work
to keep the Valley Springs-Sioux Falls-Mitchell trackage
in tip top shape. (Leonard Tripp collection)

Ah, Mitchell! Home to not only the world's only Corn Palace, but an important yard and terminal for the Milwaukee. The yearly Corn Palace celebration in the fall brought visitors in to town for a festival to celebrate the harvest. Country folk were astonished by the modern-looking Main Street as they strolled up from the classic Milwaukee station at the end of the street. Mitchell was the Milwaukee's town, even though the Omaha/North Western ran a branch line in from Sioux Falls. (Courtesy of Julia Geiman; SD State Historical Society)

MILWAUKEE DEPOT MITCHELL

Sioux Falls became the home of the most extensive street railway system in the state. Four companies operated horse drawn and electric streetcars from the late 1880's until 1929. The South Dakota Rapid Transit and Railway Company operated this interesting set of ornate interurban cars out to East Sioux Falls at the turn of the century. The smartly attired conductor worked for the Sioux Falls Traction System, the last line to operate in the city. (Four photos, Leonard Tripp collection)

Other cities caught the streetcar craze, as in this view of the Huron Street Railway, which only lasted from 1886 until 1890. (Leonard Tripp collection)

A Great Northern 0-6-0 yard "goat" and its crew at Sioux Falls. (Leonard Tripp collection)

The North Western's Aberdeen depot. (R.C. Lathrop collection)

Opening on Thanksgiving Day, 1910, the Aberdeen Street Railway served the city until 1932. The line is prominent in this view of Aberdeen in the bustling teens. (Leonard Tripp collection)

The Milwaukee's first station in Aberdeen. (Leonard Tripp collection)

The Great Northern built this small, but stately brick structure at the end of its Huron branch. (R.C. Lathrop collection)

Down the street in Huron, the North Western's yards dominated the north end of the city. (courtesy of Greg Walters)

A Rock Island train pauses at the White depot on a southbound run down from Watertown.

From the coaling tower, the photographer captures a rare view of the Milwaukee's ten-stall roundhouse and turntable in Madison. Lines to Bristol and to Wessington Springs were serviced out of Madison as well as out to the main line at Flandreau. (SD State Historical Society)

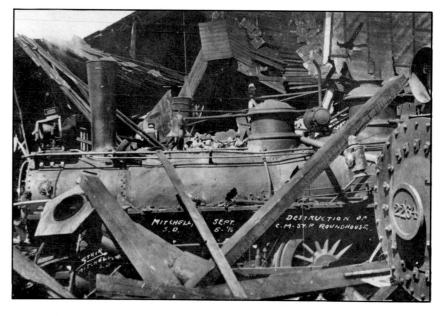

A fire in the machine shop of the Milwaukee's roundhouse in Mitchell on September 5, 1916 damaged more than the structure, as this view depicts. (SD State Historical Society)

An interesting view of the back of the joint C&NW/Omaha depot at Salem. The angle of the depot was designed to fit at the crossing of the North Western's Hawarden, Iowa - Iroquois, South Dakota line and the Omaha's Sioux Falls to Mitchell line.

A Milwaukee passenger train blasts out of Elk Point for Sioux City. Note the enclosed octagonal water tank beyond the depot. It is possibly the only one of its kind constructed in the state.

North Western 4-4-0 #684 pauses with its train at an unknown station on the Yankton line. The branch left the C&NW main at Centerville to reach the city in 1884. (Leonard Tripp collection)

A Milwaukee wedge plow is about to shower the Dell Rapids depot in this 1918 photo.

The famous Milwaukee bridge over the Dells at Dell Rapids.

North Western 4-6-0 #1226 waits to depart from Union Station in Hot Springs in this photo from 1915. The Burlington and the North Western shared this sandstone station until the North Western's line to Buffalo Gap was washed out, and abandoned in the thirties. (courtesy of James Ehernberger)

Rock Island 4-6-0 #1501 and crew pose in Sioux Falls, circa 1915. (Leonard Tripp collection)

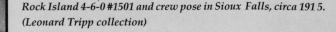

RAILROAD TIME TABLES

ROCK ISLAND.

	Leaves	Arrives
Chicago Pass*	3.00 pm	11:30 am
Daylight special	6:10 am	9:00 pm
Chicago freight	5:35 pm	10:00 am
Chicago freight	6:30 am	4:45 pm

*Daily with through sleeper.

C., M. & St. P. RY.

Southbound—		Arrive.
Aberdeen & St. Paul		12:50 pm
St. Paul & La Crosse		3:40 pm
		Depart
Sioux City & Omaha		7:20 am
Chamberlain, Mitchell and Aberdeen		11:00 am
Chicago & Milwaukee		1:00 pm
Mitchell		6:40 pm
Northbound—		Arrive.
Mitchell		10:15 am
Chicago & Sioux City		1:35 pm
Chamberlain, Mitchell and Aberdeen		2:55 pm
Sioux City & Omaha		5:30 pm
		Depart
St. Paul & La Crosse		10:20 am
Aberdeen & St. Paul		1:35 pm
Sunday Trains—		Depart
Chicago & Milwaukee		11:15 am
		Arrive
Chicago & Milwaukee		1:25 pm

C., ST. P., M. & O.

	Leaves	Arrives.
St. Paul Pass	11:15 am	6:20 am
St. Paul Pass	9:15 pm	5:50 pm
Mitchell Pass*	6:30 am	11:10 am
Mitchell Pass	5:55 pm	10:05 pm
Salem Acc'n	11:10 am	2:55 pm
Salem Acc'n	3:15 pm	9:15 am

*Daily.

Omaha Road 4-6-0 #306 poses alongside the Sioux Falls roundhouse with a collection of shop workers. Most later Omaha engines were built to North Western standards, due to the latter's controlling interest of the Omaha. (Leonard Tripp collection)

The unusual Illinois Central depot at Rowena (Leonard Tripp collection)

A high-stepping Illinois Central 4-4-0 poses at the East Sioux Falls depot with a justifiably proud crew. (Leonard Tripp collection)

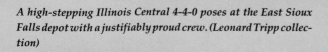

No trains for a while, on the North Western at Piedmont. The narrow-gauge cars in the right portion of the photo belong to the Burlington Route. The line from Piedmont from Lead was originally built in 1890 by the Black Hills and Fort Pierre, and then taken over by the Burlington in 1901. (R.C. Lathrop collection)

A narrow-gauge Warren-Lamb Lumber yard geared steamer is pictured west of Fairburn on the Company's line to Custer State Park. The line connected up with the North Western at Fairburn, where logs off the narrow gauged cars were loaded on the standard-gauge North Western cars for a ride to Warren-Lamb Sawmill in Rapid City. This operation lasted from 1917 until 1927.

Freighters delivered the goods from the railheads to the farms
and ranches of the West River Country until the arrival of autos
and roads. Here, a pioneer freighter in the New Underwood area,
William Crosbie poses with his team. Also, Chris Hilmer of New
Underwood provided transportation of coal and goods to the
area. Both were the maternal great-grandfathers of the author.

Once a few of the new contraptions called autos came, they
began to displace the teams and wagons. Here, an early Ford
truck is used by Jess Mills of Hermosa to transport coal as well
as the U.S. Mail. You guessed it, my great-grandfather. Did I
mention that he also was the editor of the Hermosa Pilot
newspaper?

The scenic standard-gauge line in the Black Hills was the Rapid City, Black Hills and Western. Both steamers and small gas-electrics took care of the passengers on the torturous 34 mile route up from Rapid City to Mystic. The line curved back and forth over Rapid Creek and smaller tributaries on 111 timber trestles in that short distance.

Also a candidate for the scenic line of the Hills was the Burlington's branch from Englewood to Spearfish.

Spearfish Canon, Black Hills, S. D.

A Milwaukee publicity photo of their new train to the West Coast, the Olympian, which went into service in May, 1911.

During the booming era of cattle shipments out of Belle Fourche in the first years of the decade, the North Western was kept busy. This view of a line of fired-up power ready to leave on stock trains is typical of the activity. Note Wyoming and North Western #1 on the point. The Wyoming and North Western was another early subsidiary of the North Western, and was the company formed to push westward from Casper, Wyoming. (SD State Historical Society)

An open coach brings up the rear of a Rapid Canyon Line train as it leaves Rapid City. The Crouch Line offered many special trips for conventions and other occasions. (courtesy of Mary Farrar)

Another view of the Crouch Line in timber territory west of Rapid, only this is a much more perilous view of early day railroading in the Hills. (courtesy of Mary Farrar)

A Crouch Line train is pulling into Hisega, the home of the Pierre Lodge. The line wrapped itself along Rapid Creek almost the entire 34 miles west of Rapid City to a junction with the Burlington's High Line at Mystic. Trains stopped along the route to let sightseers, picnickers, and fishermen off to enjoy the sights, and would then pick them up on the way back. All in all, the ideal short line. (courtesy of Mary Farrar)

WARNING!
DON'T FAIL TO MAKE THE
TRIP THROUGH
ROYAL GORGE
OF THE BLACK HILLS
DAILY TRAIN SERVICE VIA
R.C.B.H.&W.R.R.
34 MILES OF THRILLS — RAPID CANYON — OBSERVATION CARS REDUCED
110 BRIDGES

Chapter Four

Familiar Problems/New Challenges

Railroad mileage in the state reached its peak in the decade of 1910 to 1920. The remaining lands of the West River Country had been claimed, the eastern part of the state had settled into a comfortable system of farming, with a scattering of towns and cities to serve them. The increasing population was primarily dependent on the agricultural economy, except in the Black Hills, where agriculture coexisted with mining, timbering, and the increasing influence of tourism.

So, the years after 1920 became a time of transition for the railroads in the state. With the injection of one four letter word into the American vocabulary, a-u-t-o, the stage was set for the rationalization of the railroad system in South Dakota.

It cannot be said that the railroads were entirely a victim of the rapid expansion of automobile travel, highway construction, and motor carrier diversion of tonnage from the rails. They did bring some of the competition on themselves, by not responding to the passengers and shippers. As in any "virtual monopoly", the railroads were not always sympathetic to the concerns of the public. They developed a certain reputation as greedy, heartless businesses that had no concern for their neighbors or customers. There were legitimate cases of fraud, rate overcharges, and corruption that befell the railroads, but as their monopolies began to erode, good and bad things began to occur.

Some smaller towns in the state began to feel the effects of this new mobility inspired by the highways. Trade centers began to develop in hub cities like Aberdeen, Watertown, Mitchell, Sioux Falls, and Rapid City. The populace of these cities seemed to be settling into a controlled existence, not losing that pioneering drive, but not gunning down cowboys in the street either. This was no more apparent than in the Black Hills. The boys in the Hills were about to hatch a scheme that would put the state on the map, and establish the foundation for the second-ranked economy in the state.

The growing number of grade crossing collisions between trains and the ever increasing number of autos led to the first "Crossing Campaign" in 1922. (Leonard Tripp collection)

After the first World War, the farm economy in the country suffered from lower prices and overexpansion. This was true in the areas of the West River area, and South Dakota Senator Peter Norbeck aimed to change the fortunes for both farmers and the state in general. He proposed a trip by President Calvin Coolidge to the Black Hills, which would give the President a view of the farming situation on the way. The President could also stay the summer in the Black Hills, a luxury afforded the chief executive before more modern times. The nation scoffed at this proposal from the Black Hills, but to the amazement of nearly all, the President accepted the invitation. South Dakota could never be the same again.

An elaborate plan was assembled for the transportation and accommodations of the President, his large staff, and a multitude of others to accompany him to the "west" for the summer. The Chicago and North Western was instructed to have a train ready in Chicago for the trip through Wisconsin, Minnesota, and central South Dakota to Rapid City. The Hills painted, polished and primped everything in just over a month after the mid-May, 1927 announcement of the visit. The road from Rapid City to Hermosa, and on to the Game Lodge, had just received its first gravel as the polished train arrived in Rapid City on June 15.

During the summer in the Hills, "Silent Cal" played tourist, and the world watched. The President caught beautiful rainbow trout, attended rodeos, worshiped in a quaint white church in Hermosa, and launched a project that would become the symbol of South Dakota. On August 10, 1927,

Joanne Halley and her grandfather James Halley pose in front of the future Shrine Of Democracy. After the dedication of the monument by President Coolidge in the summer of 1927, the faces began to emerge from the granite. The outline of Washington is just beginning to develop in this photo. (courtesy of Joan Lintz)

Burlington trolley #12151 cruises down the center of Lead in the early twenties. With the competition from the autos, the electric interurbans made their final trips between Lead and Deadwood in 1924. (Leonard Tripp collection)

The last streetcar to operate in South Dakota is pictured on its last day of service in Sioux Falls - August 18, 1929. The trolley system in the city served the downtown area as well as lines out to the college district in the western part of the city and to East Sioux Falls. (Leonard Tripp collection)

Coolidge, Senator Norbeck, dignitaries, and an anxious crowd of onlookers climbed the base of a mountain of granite near Keystone. Named for a New York businessman, the piece of granite called Rushmore was dedicated that day. The President presented the first drill bits to a man who would also change the state forever, Gutzon Borglum.

Coolidge pledged the government's support of Borglum's Shrine of Democracy during the dedication, and that pledge kept the project on line. Gradually over the following years until the monument's completion in 1941, the profiles of Washington, Jefferson, Roosevelt, and Lincoln took shape against the Black Hills sky. The vision of Norbeck, state historian Doane Robinson, the President, and of Borglum also became a vision for the state. It also became a bright spot in the depression years of the twenties and the "Dirty Thirties" for the state.

The evolution of travel had become a factor in the survival for not only small towns in the state, but of the branch lines through rural South Dakota. Mining in the Black Hills was on the downturn, and the majority of the railroads in the Hills were fading or gone by 1930. This left the Hills with a Burlington line from Edgemont to Deadwood and Lead, and the North Western skirting the eastern slopes on its way to Deadwood and Belle Fourche. Gone were the narrow gauge lines, the spurs lost to flooding to Spearfish(CB&Q) and Hot Springs(C&NW), and the interurban trolley between Lead and Deadwood. The eastern parts of the state began to lose branches in the middle years of the thirties. Cuts had to be made during this time, as the depression had claimed some of the agriculturally-dependent systems as victims. Caught in receivership were the North Western, Rock Island, Soo Line, and the Minneapolis and St. Louis, while the Burlington and Great Northern made it barely by.

As for the Milwaukee, it had been in bankruptcy since 1925 for all practical purposes. It had come under reorganization in 1927, when the name was lengthened to the Chicago, Milwaukee, St. Paul and Pacific. The heavy debt incurred in the Pacific extension, the tight competition on the western route, and the weak agricultural economy dealt a one-two-three punch to the railroad. The 1927 effort lasted only into 1932, when the line again filed for protection. The Milwaukee finally pulled out of the receivership in 1945. The railroads all profited from the traffic upturn during the Second World War, but time was about to catch up with the state's lines.

While the thirties had brought about the end of a great share of the branch line passenger trains, the railroads were still obliged to run others. The relative prosperity in the post-war years allowed the North Western and the Milwaukee to launch new services in the state. The Milwaukee's Olympian Hiawatha, a Chicago to Seattle streamliner, was introduced in 1947. The sleek orange train whistled over the main line through Aberdeen and Mobridge behind streamlined steam locomotives and eventually diesels. The North Western inaugurated service of the Dakota 400 from Chicago to Huron in the spring of 1950. The dieselized train was extended to Rapid City in the mid-fifties to service the tourist trade of the Black Hills, but the tide was going against the railroad attempts to keep the passenger trains in operation.

An Illinois Central 2-6-0 backs a circus train into a yard track in the late twenties. (Leonard Tripp collection)

The decade of the 1960's brought the final runs of passenger trains in the state, as well as the beginning of large abandonment programs by the railroads. In 1960, the remaining passenger trains were:

The Dakota 400; Rapid City, Pierre, Huron to Chicago(C&NW)
The Olympian Hiawatha; Pacific Coast, Mobridge, Aberdeen, Minneapolis, Chicago(MILW)
The Arrow; Sioux Falls, Canton to Chicago(MILW)
Trains 41 & 42; Omaha to Billings, via Edgemont(CB&Q)
Trains 15 & 16, Watertown to Minneapolis(gas-electric motorcar - M&StL)

Gone from the scene in 1960 was the Minneapolis and St. Louis, taken over in a corporate merger with the North Western. The decade would not only be the era of abandonments, but of the merger. Talks between the North Western and the Milwaukee of a possible merger persisted for several years, but never came of any kind of solution. After they parted, the Milwaukee began to seek inclusion in a merger between the Milwaukee's competitors to the West Coast, the Great Northern and the Northern Pacific, plus the Burlington Route. The Milwaukee could not come to terms with the future Burlington Northern either, although the other three and the Spokane, Portland and Seattle Railroad merged

on March 2, 1970.

The Milwaukee was suffering, even though certain provisions were made into the Burlington Northern merger for new Milwaukee interchanges. The Milwaukee was also not abandoning branches at the pace of the line's primary state competition, the North Western. The Milwaukee was nearing the proverbial "end of the line".

However, the Burlington Northern was booming. West of the Black Hills in eastern Wyoming, the BN ran through a basin of virtually untapped coal fields. The early 1970's found this source in high demand, and the BN's coal bonanza was just beginning. Unit train, after unit coal train, rolled out on the main line through Edgemont, once a sleepy little cattle town on the southwestern slope of the Hills. In those days, three or four trains passed through daily, plus a train to or from Deadwood, and that was the size of it. Almost overnight, as many as 60 trains a day turned Edgemont into a bustling place. Some coal and other overhead traffic also began to roll up the ex-Great Northern main from Omaha to the Twin Cities via Garretson. The "Big Nuthin'" was OK, the Milwaukee was not.

On December 19, 1977, the Milwaukee again filed for reorganization under the U.S. bankruptcy law. Under a part of the reorganization, the Milwaukee's trustee requested authority to abandon all lines in South Dakota. He was granted that eventually, but was to retain the main line through

114

A depression-era freight train is led eastbound out of Rapid City by two class R 4-6-0's in this view by photographer Otto Perry on September 3, 1933. The 42-car train is at MP 643 of the PRC(Pierre-Rapid City) line. (Otto Perry photo, Western History Department-Denver Public Library)

The next day, Mr. Perry travelled into the Black Hills and caught Burlington 2-6-6-2 #4107 on a train bound for Deadwood on the scenic "High Line." Out of view at the rear of the train is sister locomotive #4106 in service as a helper on the grades to Deadwood. The train is dropping down a 3 percent grade here towards Mystic, the junction with the Rapid City, Black Hills and Western Railroad; the Crouch Line. (Otto Perry photo, WHD-DPL)

to Miles City, Montana and the Milbank to Sisseton branch line. That modified plan was approved on November 1, 1979, and the last trains ran out their time in final trips over the various state lines in the following months into early 1980.

At this point in South Dakota's railroad history (1980), the state had lost fully 60 percent of the railroad service from its peak in 1911. Drastic events often require drastic measures, and the 1980's would definitely bring those.

Later on September 4th, Otto caught train #43 arriving at Edgemont. During the depression, the gas electric and coach were sufficient equipment for the service. (Otto Perry photo, WHD-DPL)

One of the most unique stories of the railroads' role in the development of the state is that of Wesleyan Church Reverend J.F. Simpson. It was at the time of the birth of his daughter Faith that his extensive use of the railroads as the President of the Dakota Conference of the Wesleyan Church was brought to the attention of Milwaukee Road officials. A few days after the pass request was submitted, it was received by Simpson. That pass was renewed annually for over forty years, as well as passes given to the Rev. Simpson by the North Western and the Great Northern that allowed the Reverend to carry on the

work of the church in the Northern Plains area. In the two vertical photos, Rev. Simpson and his wife Vena are shown at Conde; J.F. (Frank) in the vestibule of the coach and Vena standing by the depot. The Reverend was on his way to Bushnell, South Dakota(on the Rock Island line southeast of Watertown) where he would serve from June to October, 1916. The inset is a photo of the Reverend Simpson, and the photo to the left is of one of the last passes issued to Simpson by the Milwaukee on his Bible. In all, the Reverend logged over 1 million miles via rail in his service to the Wesleyan Church and to the Lord.

Mr. Perry made numerous trips to South Dakota during the thirties from his home in Denver, and on March 17, 1935 made this exposure of Train #141 leaving Edgemont behind 4-6-0 #968 bound for Deadwood. (Otto Perry photo, WHD-DPL)

The Rapid City, Black Hills and Western Railroad fought with the elements, the creditors, and numerous other setbacks in its history that began in 1893. The railroad was finally abandoned in 1947. It derived its nickname "The Crouch Line" from one of its presidents that fought to keep the line in operation. As it fought to continue operational, it fielded a wide variety of locomotives and equipment on its

RAPID CITY, BLACK HILLS & WESTERN RAILROAD COMPANY
RAPID CITY, SOUTH DAKOTA

roster. Views in this collage of the "mighty" Crouch Line are of the Rapid City depot, a train snaking its way along Rapid Creek in Dark Canyon, a motorcar and trailer in passenger service near Silver City, and the cover of a promotional booklet distributed in the 1930's. (courtesy of Rapid City Public Library, Leonard Tripp, SD State Historical Society)

HISTORY
of
The Crookedest Railroad on Earth

Rapid Canyon Line

GENERAL OFFICES
Rapid City, South Dakota

119

A wayfreight pauses at the Rapid City station, again for the camera of Otto Perry. The cars in the background are on the transfer track for the Crouch Line. (Otto Perry photo, WHD-DPL)

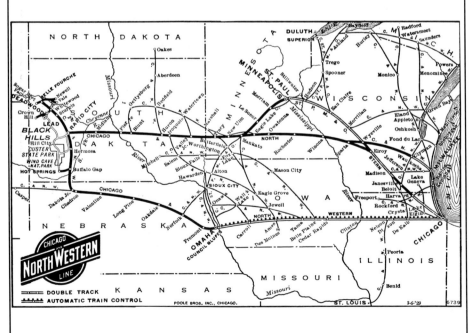

DIRECT ROUTES TO THE BLACK HILLS

The Chicago & North Western Ry. followed the original trails and was the first railroad to reach the Black Hills. In the operation of its passenger service in and out of the Black Hills, the North Western provides splendid through trains, modernly equipped with every convenience for the safety and comfort of its patrons.

HOMESEEKERS TICKETS—For just $2.00 more than the regular one-way fare you can buy round-trip Homeseekers tickets from Chicago and points east of the Missouri River to any destination in the Black Hills district. On sale and

good going each Tuesday during the year. They are good for stopover at any intermediate point in the Homeseekers territory. Return limit 21 days from date of sale.

SUMMER TOURIST TICKETS—Daily June 1 to September 30, round-trip Summer Tourist tickets are on sale to the Black Hills at unusually low-fares, from all points in the United States east of and including the Missouri River, also certain territory west of the Missouri River. Stopovers at any point en route. Final return limit October 31, year of issue.

Write agent for further information, or address the following C. & N. W. Ry. agencies:

RAPID CITY, S. D.—R. L. Hall, *Agent*—E. E. Benjamin, *General Agent*

C. A. CAIRNS, *Passenger Traffic Manager* — 400 W. Madison St., Chicago

A. R. GOULD, *Asst. Pass. Traffic Mgr.*   R. THOMSON, *Asst. Pass. Traffic Mgr.*   M. R. LEAHY, *Gen'l Pass. Agent*

Chicago & North Western Railway

A-598-29-15M   ALCO-GRAVURE, INC. Chicago

A Minneapolis and St. Louis class H-1 2-8-0 rides the turntable in Watertown in the thirties. Locomotive #405 was built in 1909, and met its fate at the mercy of the scrapper's torch in 1946. (Codington County Historical Society, Watertown)

As the thirties saw the downfall of passenger train service on most lines in the state other than on the select main trunk lines, the gas-electrics began to hold down more assignments. A North Western motor is making a stop at the Lebanon depot before continuing on through Gettysburg to Blunt.

A Great Northern steam rotary plow is on loan to the Minneapolis and St. Louis in this photo at Crocker, northwest of Watertown. (Codington County Historical Society, Watertown)

Two of the terminals that served the railroads were Mobridge(top) and Huron. As the jumping off point of the Pacific extension, Mobridge was an important staging yard through the years. The Huron roundhouse was only a part of the yard action, as trains were made up and broken down here for the various lines that radiated out from the city. (collections of R.C. Lathrop, Bob Eddy)

One of the North Western's class Z 2-8-0's rests alongside the roundhouse at Huron. (Greg Walters collection)

Chicago, Rock Island and Pacific train #419 rolls into Sioux Falls after its run in from Chicago. (Leonard Tripp collection)

Milwaukee 4-6-0 #2860 heads up a four car train #3, the Sioux, into Rapid City on June 21, 1936. (Otto Perry photo, WHD-DPL)

An Omaha 4-6-0 and crew in Sioux Falls. (Leonard Tripp collection)

Illinois Central 4-6-0 #5034 and train #611 after its arrival in Sioux Falls from Fort Dodge, Iowa. (Leonard Tripp collection)

Chicago and North Western train #411, the Minnesota and Black Hills Express, heads into Rapid City on the morning of June 21, 1936. One of the North Western's classy Atlantic class 4-4-2's powers the seven car train past the camera at a photographer-estimated 55 MPH. (Otto Perry photo, WHD- DPL)

A combination baggage/coach car brings up the rear of this mixed train eastbound out of Mobridge in 1938. (Otto Perry photo, WHD-DPL)

A Milwaukee 2-8-2 heads an eastbound freight near Selby on August 13, 1938. Note the bundles of snow fences on either side of the tracks, as winter is never far away in South Dakota. (Otto Perry photo, WHD-DPL)

Also on August 13, 1938, the Milwaukee's crack train to the coast in the pre-Olympian Hiawatha days rolls east between Mobridge and Aberdeen. Train #15, the Olympian, is powered by Baltic class 4-6-4 #142. Before the diesel era, the 4-6-4's were the preferred power on the Olympian between Minneapolis and Harlowton, Montana. (Otto Perry photo, WHD-DPL)

A variation of the Baltic class were six equipped with a streamlined orange and maroon cowling to match their trains. Here in Aberdeen, one of the first of the racehorses is being viewed by a large crowd shortly after their delivery in mid-1938. These engines commonly clocked in at over 100 MPH, and were capable of hitting 120 MPH. They were often used on the main line through Aberdeen, as well as on secondary trains using the Aberdeen-Mitchell-Sioux City line. (Brown County Historical Society)

A colorized postcard of the Shrine of Democracy, completed in 1941.

A Colorado and Southern 4-6-0 is ready to depart Deadwood with the daily passenger consist for Edgemont in July 1941. The Burlington leased several of the C&S ten-wheelers over the years for service in the Black Hills. (collection of James L. Ehernberger)

129

A Minneapolis and St. Louis train treads lightly over the line to Aberdeen during flooding of the James River near Stratford in 1943. (Codington County Historical Society, Watertown)

A Great Northern steamer poses in front of the Watertown depot, circa 1943. (Codington County Historical Society, Watertown)

The Milwaukee agent poses by his agency in Plankington. Note the double water towers on the line.

A view from the tender at the consist of an eastbound "Sioux" between Mitchell and Canton. (A.C. Roman collection)

131

A local train arrives at the Canton depot. Canton was a mighty busy place in the morning, with trains in from Chicago and the east, the branch from Sioux Falls to the north, the line to Sioux City southward, and the trains from Aberdeen, Mitchell, and Rapid City on the west line. (Leonard Tripp collection)

DAD, WHERE DO THE TRACKS GO?

"SON, if you walked those tracks west, you'd walk into a country so big you'd feel about knee high to a grasshopper.

"You'd see Indians sure—and cowboys, too—but you'd see lots of other things. Miles and miles of grain, more sheep than you ever counted—cattle galore; sky-scrapin' mountains that look like they had a hunk of ice cream on top of 'em.

"You'd see rushin' water turnin' factory wheels and changin' yellow waste country to land as green as our pasture; apples half as big as your head and trees as tall as Jack's bean stalk. You'd meet friendly people, livin' on farms and ranches and in up-and-comin' towns

and cities that ain't much older than you, as towns go.

"Finally, you'd wind up lookin' out over the Pacific Ocean—lookin' west to where your brother Jim is with his Marine outfit. Yes sir, if you'd walk those tracks west, you'd see a powerful lot of what Jim's fightin' for."

★　★　★

The Milwaukee Road tracks lead to new opportunities. You can choose your climate and scenery—the type of endeavor you're fitted for. Live in old established communities or pioneer in "young" country. If you're thinking of making a move in the post-war days look to the west and northwest!

11,000-MILE SUPPLY LINE FOR WAR AND HOME FRONTS

A "Louie" crew and family members pose next to a M&StL gas-electric car on the Watertown turntable. (Codington County Historical Society, Watertown)

One of the more touching stories of Dakota railroading is that of the "Little Fellow's Grave". A boy, whose parents were a part of a maintenance crew on the North Western between Watertown and Redfield, died of small pox in August 1888. A man named "Big Bill" Chambers worked as a brakeman on the ballasting train, and was one of the few friends of the boy. When the boy died, the section crew fashioned a coffin from scrap lumber on the train. As the nearest undertaker was miles away, the body was interred next to the railroad line. But shortly after the boy's death, the parents disappeared. The following Decoration Day(1889), Big Bill began a forty-year tradition of taking flowers to the grave and maintaining it. After the death of Bill Chambers in 1931, North Western crews carried on the tradition along with local residents. The traditional observance continues today, with a service on Memorial Day each year. (courtesy of Bert Moritz, Clark County Courier)

The almost yearly battle with the drifts put the crews and the equipment to the test. Here a M&StL mixed train plows through the cuts of snow between Wallace and Bradley in the winter of 1948. (Codington County Historical Society, Watertown)

The battle by the North Western, M&StL, and Milwaukee to open lines during and after the "Blizzard of `49". (courtesy of Jim Walker, Johnny Severson, Lowell Shuck)

SCENE ON N.W.R.R.
WALL, S. DAK. BLIZZARD
— 1949 —

North Western E-7 #5018 is given the honor of the only C&NW diesel to be named by the railroad as it receives the Dakota 400 lettering prior to its maiden run. The train began service to Huron on April 30, 1950, and was greeted in Huron the day before by a large crowd curious to see "their" streamliner. (courtesy of the Chicago and North Western Transportation Co.)

Milwaukee 4-6-0 #1163 arrives at Milbank with a train off the Sisseton branch on August 21, 1949.

The end for the steamers was at hand by the early 1950's, and pictured here is the last steam on the Watertown to Huron GN Line in 1951. Shown left is fireman Leo Huston and to the right is engineer Alvin Brevig. (Codington County Historical Society, Watertown)

C&NW train #514 arrives in Brookings on a cold morning in January, 1951. (collection of Steve Friezen)

Inside the Brookings depot on that -15 degree morning in 1951, telegrapher Bob Carey and Agent Howard Grahm discuss the day's train movements. (collection of Steve Friezen)

Agent Grahm hands the orders to the conductor of Train #21, bound from Brookings to Watertown. The conductor then gives the engineer the "Highball" signal. (collection of Steve Friezen)

The crew of Brookings-Watertown train #21 pauses at Sioux Valley Junction to take on water, and then curve northwest on the Watertown branch. Note the refrigerator cars behind the engine-destined for the Swift Packing Company at Watertown no doubt. (collection of Steve Friezen)

The Iron Horses are about to be put out into pasture, as these views of the last steamer on the Milwaukee at Mitchell, and on the Omaha/North Western in Sioux Falls, circa mid 1950's. (Leonard Tripp collection)

Milwaukee 4-6-0 #1065 leads a mixed train through Canton in the fifties. Time was running out for the steamers as well as for the mixed and passenger trains of the state. Note the lightweight coach-Railway Post Office-baggage car behind the steamer. (Leonard Tripp collection)

The last mixed train on the Omaha/North Western leaves Sioux Falls eastbound. (Leonard Tripp collection)

North Western ten-wheeler #444 was retired after being the last steamer to operate on the Black Hills Division. It was sent to be a static display at the fledgling Black Hills Central tourist railroad at Hill City in 1958, where it is shown. It was sold to the Forney Transportation Museum in Denver in the late 1960's, where it remains today.

The Burlington's trains 42 and 43(shown at Edgemont in the late fifties) grazed the southwesternmost part of the state. These trains provided service between Lincoln, Nebraska and Billings, Montana until 1969. (Otto Perry photo, WHD-DPL)

Milwaukee #15, the Olympian Hiawatha, accelerates out of Bowman, North Dakota on its way to Lemmon, McLaughlin, Mobridge, Java, Aberdeen, Webster, Milbank, and points east in this Otto Perry photo from July 10, 1956. Diesel unit F-7 #101C leads the lengthy train on this day. (Otto Perry photo, WHD-DPL)

After the 1955 extension of the Dakota 400 to Rapid City, the combined train often consisted of a large number of head-end baggage and mail cars, as in this photo by Otto Perry in 1956. Diesel model E-6A #5006B leads the "400" today. (Otto Perry photo, WHD-DPL)

A bird's eye view of Pollock on the Soo Line. The town was abandoned and moved to a hill near the original site as the waters of the new Oahe Reservoir rose. The Soo adjusted its line to reach the new town, which was completed by 1962. The Soo Line depot and elevator are visible over the grazing cow. (SD State Historical Society)

F units again lead a train, this time on the North Western at Rapid City. The four-unit lashup is powering a train of Nebraska sugar beets to the U&I processing mill at Belle Fourche.

An E-7 leads the last westbound Dakota 400 out of Midland on its way to Rapid City on October 24, 1960. With the final eastbound run the following day, the North Western was out of the passenger business in South Dakota.

A set of Milwaukee F units rest in Sioux Falls between freight assignments in the early 1960's. (Leonard Tripp photo)

A Burlington brakeman is protecting the crossing at Keystone as SD-9's #457 and 437 switch cars on July 27, 1964. (photo by Robert Larson, Sioux Falls)

CB&Q train #43 has a special car tagging along on August 2, 1964. The ex-Burlington observation car was bought by the Intermountain Chapter of the National Railway Historical Society in Denver, and is heading for Deadwood for a special trip over the High Line. (James L. Ehernberger photo)

A Rock Island GP-9 idles between assignments in Sioux Falls. (Leonard Tripp photo)

A GN GP-9 shuffles cars as a special Shriners' train is assembled in Sioux Falls (Leonard Tripp photo)

Chicago and North Western roundhouse in Sioux Falls, 1966. (Leonard Tripp photo)

The "intersection" in Sioux Falls, 1967. (Leonard Tripp photo)

Rock Island variety in Sioux Falls in the 1960's. The lash-up of an F-7 and an Alco PA, combined with one of the Rock's unique outside-braced cabooses makes for a definitely interesting photo. Also, a shot of a lone GP-9 resting on the antiquated turntable in Sioux Falls is worth a frame of film. Finally, a new-image yellow and red Rock Island GP-9 and caboose pose at the Sioux Falls station. (three photos by Leonard Tripp)

The last Milwaukee Arrow is about to leave Sioux Falls in this view on September 16, 1965. The Milwaukee's yards and engine house are in the background. Below, the last Arrow leaves southbound for Chicago. (Leonard Tripp photos)

By the middle 1960's, a depot that remained was the exception to the norm. The following pages give a few glimpses of some of the holdouts of that era, including the following: Interior (MILW), Herreid and Rosholt(SOO), Strandburg and Aberdeen(M&StL/C&NW), Yankton(GN), Mitchell(Omaha/C&NW), and Clear Lake(RI). (courtesy of R.C. Lathrop, SD State Historical Society)

The rear end of train #43 at Edgemont in 1966. Note the loading of cream cans into the side door caboose on the left. The caboose for the Deadwood train still does a little rear-end business along the High Line. (photo by Robert Larson, Sioux Falls)

Four North Western GP's rest in Belle Fourche before returning to Rapid City with a train of bentonite in August, 1967. (photo by A.J. Wolff)

The same day, Mr. Wolff caught a Milwaukee SD-9 resting at the Rapid City roundhouse before an evening run through the Badlands to Murdo.

The Republican Party chartered a Milwaukee train in 1968 to stump for its slate of candidates. For the most part, it worked for them. (Leonard Tripp photos)

An Illinois Central GP-10 rebuild is at Sioux Falls in the spring of 1969. A comprehensive rebuilding program was begun on IC GP's in 1968, and this project gave the locomotives an extended life. (Leonard Tripp photo)

By the early 1970's, the Omaha/C&NW roundhouse at Sioux Falls had fallen on hard times. (Chuck Park collection)

158

As the North Western began to wind down operations of its Deadwood branch in the late 1960's the freight house/depot began to look run down. Compare it with a view from the 1890's with the Elkhorn 4-4-0 at the platform. The last seventy years or so had taken a toll on the structure. (Centennial Archives, Deadwood Public Library)

The new kid on the block - Burlington Northern. Formed in 1970 with the merger of the Burlington, the Great Northern, Northern Pacific, and the Spokane, Portland and Seattle railroads, the BN became the largest railroad in the country. A northbound BN freight to Deadwood is led by an ex-CB&Q SD-9, still in Chinese red and gray, near the Crazy Horse Monument in 1974. (Larry Dilts photo)

Shortly after the BN's creation, the coal boom began in eastern Wyoming. A set of BN's General Electric U30-Cs head up a west-bound hopper train at Edgemont on June 27, 1975. The fresh ballast under the new ribbon rails is just one sign of the rapid expansion of tonnage and traffic on this line. (James L. Ehernberger photo)

The graceful lines of American Freedom Train(Southern Pacific) GS-4 #4449 are evident in this view on September 6, 1975 in Canton. The Freedom Train's Bicentennial tour of the country brought it up the Milwaukee to a display in Sioux Falls at the W.H. Lyon fairgrounds. (Leonard Tripp collection)

E-2-74 500M

FORM 214 REV.

Chicago, Milwaukee, St. Paul and Pacific Railroad Company

CLEARANCE

STATION Canton _____ Sept 6, 19 75

To C&E Extra Sp 4449 West _____

Clearance No. _____ To _____
(This line to be used in connection with Rule 85 or Rule 97(A)

I have 6 orders for your train.

No. 13 No. 14 No. 15 No. 149 No. 50 404

No. ___ No. ___ No. ___ No. ___ No. ___

No. ___ No. ___ No. ___ No. ___ No. ___

Do not leave before _____
(This line to be used when required as prescribed by Rule 91(A)

OK 1031 am R Lm Konutzko
TIME SUPERINTENDENT OPERATOR

AND WHISTLE FREELY WHEN APPROACHING AND PASSING
ALL POINTS BETWEEN CANTON AND SIOUX FALLS
WHERE CROWDS OF PEOPLE CAN BE EXPECTED
ON OR NEAR TRACKS TO VIEW FREEDOM TRAIN AS IT
PASSES ALL TRAINS BETWEEN THESE POINTS MUST BE
OPERATED UNDER CONTROL AND STOP IF NECESSARY TO
AVOID STRIKING PEOPLE GATHERED TO VIEW FREEDOM TRAIN
FREEDOM TRAIN IS EXPECTED TO LEAVE CANTON ABOUT
1045 AM AND ARRIVE SIOUX FALLS AT 1130 AM

RLM

The end of an era at Winner in June 1978 as the last North Western train heads down the track. (photo by Rosebud Photo Company of Winner)

Oh yea, but was it still #1? By the fall of 1978, the Milwaukee had entered its final bankruptcy, and a GP-20 heads through Sioux Falls toward Canton. (Leonard Tripp photo)

A set of Milwaukee F units rests by the Aberdeen roundhouse in the winter of 1978-1979. (photo by David B. Miller)

To compound the Milwaukee's woes in the winter of 1979-1980, power shortages required the leasing of a number of diesels, including Canadian National SD-40's seen here at Ipswich. (photo by David B. Miller)

The Milwaukee gave up on the Faith branch in 1979, and the Faith depot looks abandoned in this view by David B. Miller.

Up the line from Aberdeen, Alco RSD-5 #1686 idles while the crew gets orders at the Oakes, North Dakota depot. The grain tonnage still moved over the light rail branches of the plains in the fleets of 40 foot box cars until the early 1980's. (Bob Eddy photo)

Burlington Northern's "antique" SW-1 switcher at Lead in the late 1970's. While the crew lunches at the cafe behind the ex-CB&Q unit, the 91 purrs as it awaits the call to duty to switch several sidings at the Homestake Gold Mine complex. (photo by Larry Dilts)

A deceptive photo of the Milwaukee Road's condition is painted by this photo of the Big Stone Power Company's coal train rolling through McIntosh in the fall of 1979. While operations on the main would remain those of the Milwaukee for a couple more years, the days were numbered for the majority of the trackage in the state as the Milwaukee prepared to abandon operations. (Ted Schnepf photo)

Chapter Five

The "New" Dakota Rails

Concern over the deepening crisis in rail transportation in the state began during the mid-1970's. The unstable nature of the railroads, especially the Milwaukee, led to the creation of the State Department of Transportation's Division of Railroads in 1975. The Division was aided in policy development from the South Dakota Railroad Advisory Commission, a five member group appointed by the Governor. The state of railroading in 1980 found the Commission with some depressing statistics to deal with.

The Milwaukee was gone, and nearly fifty percent of the operational trackage in the state had been abandoned in that bankruptcy. The Rock Island was gone by the early 1970's, and the Illinois Central was in the process of abandoning its single line into Sioux Falls. Soo Line continued to operate its two marginal branches in the northern part of the state. The North Western trackage in the state was at best adequate, except for its north-south line along the Black Hills. The Burlington Northern trackage in the state ranged from passable to great, but only served the western and extreme eastern areas of the state.

Spurred by the rail crisis, the 1980 State Legislature authorized the purchase of up to 1,254 miles of rail facilities. The law was signed into effect on March 14, 1980. The lines to be purchased were those deemed essential to the state's transportation network. The legislature also created the South Dakota Railroad Authority to "plan, establish, acquire, develop, construct, purchase, enlarge, maintain, equip, and protect railroad facilities deemed necessary to the State." A total of 834.5 miles of Milwaukee trackage slated to be abandoned were purchased, and another 303 miles of local option lines. Funding for this purchase was secured with a temporary one percent sales tax increment on all items except food. The primary trackage purchased was the "Core System", which consisted of the Aberdeen to Sioux City line through Yankton, and the

Sioux Falls to Chamberlain line through Canton and Mitchell. The main line through from Miles City to Big Stone City was acquired in July, 1982, and also was to be operated by the Burlington Northern Railroad. The state had already signed an agreement to have the Core system operated in conjunction with other BN lines in the state.

To upgrade the trackage for continued use, the BN asked the state to put forth monies in the form of track rehabilitation instead of subsidies to the railroad. The bonds secured by the state in the purchase of the northern main line were to be retired by the Burlington Northern. The main line through Aberdeen was put back in service on April 20, 1982, with the BN providing service even though a final agreement was three months away on the purchase of the line. One of the major clauses in both

BN contracts with the state is the option for the railroad to purchase the lines when the debts are paid off.

The last section of trackage that was operated on by the Milwaukee by the end of 1982 was into Milbank. The Milwaukee was still in receivership, but operational east of this point. They interchanged cars with the new Dakota Rail Railway, the operator of the former-Milwaukee branch to Sisseton. The maverick Dakota Rail was to set the tone for the wave of short line operators to take up part of the slack in a post-Milwaukee South Dakota.

While Dakota Rail was the exception to the norm by actually forming a corporation and buying the branch, it did make sense. Other lines were created to provide service over the state-owned lines, the first being Dakota and Iowa. The line

existed to haul quarried products from the L.G. Everist quarry at Dell Rapids to Sioux City, Iowa over trackage rights from Sioux Falls south. The company bought the trackage from Sioux Falls to Dell Rapids to secure an outlet for the traffic.

An old name was resurrected for a new operation on the state-owned branch from the core system at Napa Junction to Platte in 1985. Enter the Dakota Southern, again! The trackage had not seen train service since the last Milwaukee train from Platte in early 1980. Unfortunately, it was more of a chore to pull the rails back out of the sod than to win back shippers. The shippers were cooperative in the reinstatement of service during the first year of operations. But rationalization was not quite finished. The North Western gave notice in 1984 that it was considering the abandonment of its trackage from Rapid City east to either Pierre or Wolsey. State officials and shippers lobbied to protect the line in light of its role in agricultural shipments across the state. The North Western management again declared the line up for abandonment in 1985, and the shippers, primarily along the Rapid City to Pierre segment, voiced their opposition. A group of investors was secured by negotiations between the North Western, government officials, and others to forge the Dakota, Minnesota and Eastern Railroad. The deal

With the demise of the Milwaukee, a number of interesting structures met their end as well. Shortly after the 1980 pullout on most of their trackage in the state, several Milwaukee engine houses were photographed by David Miller, then a member of the South Dakota Railroad Board.

An interesting facet of railroad history and its preservation is the railroad enthusiast, or the railfan. These "dedicated" persons of nearly every persuasion and vocation collect, photograph, discuss, and build models of their favorite railroad for both fun and profit. Here, one of western South Dakota's most knowledgeable and hospitable railroad "enthusiasts", Al Roman, seemingly is posing a BN C30-7 and its crew at Edgemont. (Greg Walters photo)

A.J. Wolff has caught four of the Burlington Northern's SD-9's and SW-1 #91 between assignments in Deadwood on February 19, 1980 in this photo. Three and four of the SD's were used from the fifties until the early 1980's to bring the trains of the Burlington and its successor Burlington Northern up the High Line from Edgemont to Deadwood, where the 91 would perform the local chores in Deadwood, Lead, and at the Kirk Power Plant.

sold the North Western's line from Rapid City to Winona, Minnesota, as well as branches to Aberdeen and Watertown. The headquarters were located in Brookings, with the line's principal locomotive and car shop at the former North Western facilities in Huron. The new railroad pledged to be customer responsive in the quest for business. Both the Dakota Southern and the DM&E immediately set forth to bring traffic back to the rails. A local company that was interested in the shippers and the cities along their respective routes; a refreshing change.

The conclusion of the DM&E sale by the North Western on September 5, 1986 signalled a new era for the state. The North Western was nearly out of the state, albeit for its lines to Sioux Falls and along the Black Hills. The Burlington Northern was now the largest carrier in the state, followed by the DM&E. The Dakota Southern gained trackage in 1987, when the BN pulled off the Mitchell to Chamberlain trackage, and the DS stepped in.

The light weight rail was well suited for light, six axle locomotives. The DS bought several ex-Milwaukee SD locomotives that had actually done time on these very lines before their initial abandonment in 1980. The Dakota Southern also created a new "subsidiary" to take over the operation of the Sisseton branch, after the Dakota Rail's exit. The new line was called the Sisseton Southern, and operated under the control of the same parent corporation of shippers and investors. Two light General Electric switchers were secured to handle the chores on the line. The partner for interchange at Milbank was not the Milwaukee any more, as the Soo Line had been the victor in 1985 in a bidding war with the North Western for the remnants of the Milwaukee.

The North Western's remaining branch into the eastern part of the state gave up the ghost in late 1988, when the line to Sioux Falls was abandoned. To fill the void, two new short lines were created. From the ex-North Western yards in downtown Sioux Falls, Ellis and Eastern provided service to the western suburb of Ellis. To the east of town, the Buffalo Ridge Railroad was formed to operate the balance of the branch into Minnesota. While the Ellis and Eastern was formed by local shippers, the Buffalo Ridge was a subsidiary of the Minnesota-

The North Western also used SD-9's on its lines across the state. A freshly painted #6602 rests at the Rapid City roundhouse with two other SD-9's on February 18, 1980. These units were used primarily eastward from Rapid City across the PRC line to Pierre and on to Huron. (A.J. Wolff photo)

Alcos reigned supreme on the North Western out of Huron until the decade of the eighties, when they were finally replaced by EMD-GP and SD's. Time is running out as RSD-5 brings a string of forty-footers up the line near Athol on September 20, 1980. (Robert P. Olmsted photo)

based Minnesota Valley Railroad. The year of 1988 also marked the resumption of service by the Dakota Southern of the former Milwaukee tracks from Chamberlain to Kadoka. Based on its prior success, the DS was ready to provide efficient service to the grain shippers along the route. Bulk commodities still could be moved via the rails more economically than over the highways, and the DS had brought that option back.

During the summer of South Dakota's centennial year, one new short line was formed. The Sisseton-Milbank Railroad took over the duties of operating the line from Milbank to Sisseton, replacing the Sisseton Southern. The state passed through the decade of the 1980's with a remarkable amount of change in the railroad system, and enters 1990 with a brighter outlook.

It almost seems that the railroads have come full circle since the early 1870's. Not only has the name of Dakota Southern been brought back, but the railroads that serve the state are feeders to larger systems around us. Barring the disputes of non-union lines that operate beyond certain regulations, the local railroads are fulfilling a need. Local lines do service the customer on a more personalized level, but even the larger railroads are beginning to realize that again. Competition brings out the worst in things sometimes, but it often gets us back to good things as well.

So, in a new decade, what are we left with? The great era of rationalization seems to have ended. Lines will undoubtedly still be sold, or abandoned, but we have a viable system in the state. The North Western is now in the process of disposition on its western line along the Black Hills, so its days are numbered. Will the DM&E acquire it? How will the Dakota Southern do on the Mitchell to Kadoka line? Does BN plan to route more traffic over the core lines from its transcontinental routes? All of these are no more than speculation, not unlike the early days of boom and bust guessing in Dakota. Maybe things haven't changed as much as we would like to think.

The best definition of history that I ever heard was summed up in one word - change. The railroads have definitely been a force in that "change."

RSD-5's #1686 and #1667 drift into the yards at Huron on a splendid day in the summer of 1980. The train just in from Aberdeen is passing a line of pulpwood gondolas bound west to the Black Hills. (Bob Eddy photo)

High-nosed RSD-5 #1688 poses as it rides the turntable at Huron in the summer of 1980. (Bob Eddy photo)

Ex-New York Central RS32 #4246 leads an RS11 and an ex-Frisco GP on train #482 at DeSmet in June 1980. After switching out a car, the train will continue on through Brookings and on into southern Minnesota. (Bob Eddy photo)

A bright, but damp, morning in September 1980 finds North Western RS32 #4243 in charge of the Watertown freight near Estelline. (Robert P. Olmsted photo)

After the abandonment of the North Western's line between Mansfield and Aberdeen in 1979, the tonnage for Aberdeen and the Oakes, ND line rode the Milwaukee/ State of SD trackage up from Wolsey. At Warner on September 21, 1980, a northbound train for Aberdeen is powered by RSD-5 #1689 and RSD-4 #1620. (Robert P. Olmsted photo)

After the legal and financial battles to secure the ex-Milwaukee lines by the state, the BN was contracted to operate the Core System. July 5, 1981 finds a very polished BN #1825 and BN business car Mississippi River at Mitchell to commemorate the reopening of service the following day. (David B. Miller photo)

A varied group of units rest near the Burlington Northern's roundhouse at Edgemont in September 1981. (A.J Wolff photo)

A westbound extra rolls over the Lance Creek bridge near Wendte on the PRC line in 1981. Wood products, cement, and quarried products made up the majority of the tonnage on the line east from Rapid City. (Ted Schnepf photo)

March 21, 1982 finds one of the last Milwaukee coal trains using the main to get to the Big Stone Power Plant at Big Stone City. Shortly, the BN would assume responsibility for the coal trains on the line. (Ted Schnepf photo)

A clean-up train operates eastward over the main line on March 21, 1982 in preparation of the line's sale to the state. A Milwaukee GP-20 leads this train of wrecked cars and empties at West Marvin. The former route of the Olympian Hiawatha has ten days until the last Milwaukee train will pass by. (Ted Schnepf photo)

Three of the Milwaukee's rare SDL-39's are the power on the last train as it pulls out of Aberdeen on March 31, 1982. (Jeff Hendricks photo)

South Dakota Governor William Janklow pounds home a symbolic spike signalling the Burlington Northern's take over of operations on the main line across the northern part of the state. (Brown County Historical Society)

Train 01X66-15 departs Andover on January 15, 1983 after picking up cars. (Jeff Hendricks photo)

Burlington Northern's Breckenridge, Minnesota local departs Aberdeen in 1982. After the BN took over the operation of the Milwaukee main, most of BN's lines in Aberdeen were abandoned and operated out of the ex-Milwaukee yards. (Jeff Hendricks photo)

A special operated over the northern main line in early April 1983 to determine the possibility of Amtrak passenger service to the state. Pictured at Mobridge on April 5th, F40PH #364 leads BN business cars Big Horn Pass, Como, and Lake Superior. The state remains as one of three in the country without Amtrak passenger service in 1990. (Jeff Hendricks photo)

Look out, here comes Dakota Rail! Formed by local shippers and former Milwaukee Road employees, Dakota Rail was the solution for service on the Milbank to Sisseton branch line. Ex-Milwaukee F-7 #81C poses in Milbank for several night photos in April 1984. Also acquired was ex-Milwaukee GP-9 #326, seen pulling past the elevators at Wilmot the next day. (three photos, Ted Schnepf)

After the abandonment of the northern end of the BN's "High Line" from Custer to Deadwood/Lead in late 1983, service was continued from Edgemont to Custer on an intermittent schedule. A northbound Custer Turn heads out of Edgemont behind an SD-9 in this view on January 2, 1985. Two empty cars and a BN waycar (caboose) trail the lone SD-9.

Extra #6637 kicks up the snow five miles west of Volga on February 22, 1986. The three SD-18's were originally owned by the Southern Railway, but joined the North Western ranks in the early 1980's for service on the central divisions. (Steve Friezen photo)

A southbound Dakota and Iowa train, led by their number 1, rolls along near McCook on May 23, 1986. The parent company of the D&I, the L.G. Everist Quarry of Dell Rapids, provides the majority of the tonnage for the railroad that runs from Dell Rapids to Sioux City, Iowa. (Ted Schnepf photo)

During an inspection trip of the Western Division in April 1986, C&NW's immaculate "Presidential F's" and their business car train rested at Rapid City. The following morning they would continue on east through to Pierre and Huron.

183

Elkton is the site for a meet between North Western's Extra #6801 East and Extra #6821 West on July 26, 1986. After the Alco era on the line east of Huron, the SD-45's and SD40-2's became common power in the days before the DM&E sale. (Steve Friezen photo)

Thursday, September 4, 1986-the last C&NW train in Brookings. The crew consisted of Frank Keach, Dean Claassen, and Gary Krick on this final run in from Watertown. The line was to become the property of the Dakota, Minnesota and Eastern Railroad Corporation the following day. (Steve Friezen photo)

Get ready to play the numbers game as we detail this unique photo by Steve Friezen on July 27, 1986. Above normal snows and rainfall brought Lake Preston to record levels in 1986, and a westbound train crosses carefully on an unusually calm day with 8 units and 102 cars. The units are: SD40-2 6859, SD-45 6473, SD-45 6568, SD40-2 6913, GP-9 4160, SD-45 6477, SD-18 6628, and SD-45 6589. The only originally-purchased North Western diesels are the SD40-2's, as the SD-45's are ex-Conrail and Burlington Northern; the GP-9 is ex-Rock Island; and the SD-18 is originally from the Southern Railway. DM&E day is about a month away.

What appears to be a North Western train is actually the first DM&E train on the Watertown branch on day two of operations - September 6, 1986. The leased C&NW GP-9 is bringing empty cement hoppers south from Watertown to Sioux Valley Junction in this view at Dempster. (Steve Friezen photo)

The fall of 1986 also saw the fall of the BN's High Line. Salvage operations on the line north of Hill City that was abandoned in 1983 were nearly finished, as well as the abandonment of the remaining trackage south from Custer to Edgemont. The final train prepares to leave Custer behind SD-9 #6181 on October 29, 1986. The trackage between Custer and Hill City was left in place, possibly to be used at some future time by a tourist railroad.

After the Milwaukee's buy out by the Soo Line, the Milwaukee units were "banditized" with the blacking out of all Milwaukee markings and renumbered. An empty coal train pulls out of the siding at Petrel on February 4, 1987 after meeting another train. (Jeff Hendricks photo)

Later on February 4, a Big Stone coal train slows for a meet at the same siding at Petrel. Three BN SD40-2's are the customary power on coal trains on the ex-Milwaukee main line. (Jeff Hendricks photo)

A meet to interchange cars at Wolsey in 1987. The BN units are on the core line south of Aberdeen, and the yet to be repainted DM&E SD-9 is on the interchange track. A cut of grain cars is to be picked off the BN for destinations on the DM&E. (Steve Friezen photo)

Dakota Southern (ex-Milwaukee) SD-9 #506 brings a 54-car unit train west through Pukwana in June 1987. Service on the Mitchell to Chamberlain line was reinstated by the BN in 1982, with the DS taking over on May 15, 1987.

DM&E GP-9 #1477 ambles up the Watertown branch near Bruce on a sultry July 31, 1987. The #1477 came to the DM&E from the Norfolk Southern, after beginning life in service for the Nickel Plate Road. (Charles Bohi photo)

The "armstrong" method of turntable operation was employed at the Sioux Falls C&NW facility in this 1987 photo by Chuck Park. The #4404 is one of the North Western's versatile GP15-1's assigned to local service throughout the midwest.

To get all eleven road diesels back to Dell Rapids after a rash of southbound trains in 1987, the Dakota and Iowa assembled this lashup consisting of numbers 6,5,20,4,21,8,2,19,3,1 and 7, plus 78 empty hoppers in tow. (Chuck Park photo)

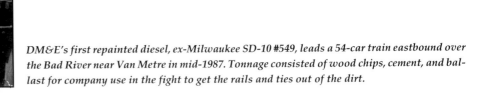

DM&E's first repainted diesel, ex-Milwaukee SD-10 #549, leads a 54-car train eastbound over the Bad River near Van Metre in mid-1987. Tonnage consisted of wood chips, cement, and ballast for company use in the fight to get the rails and ties out of the dirt.

The DM&E's eastbound "Lakota Expediter" roars upgrade out of Rapid City in the summer of 1987 behind a leased Soo Line(ex-Milwaukee) SDL-39 and three other units. North Western Vice President Alex Johnson's namesake hotel is seen over the right of the diesel. Johnson began his career on the C&NW as a telegrapher's apprentice, and became an agent at Raymond, SD in the mid-1880's. He rose through the C&NW ranks to attain the Vice Presidency in the 1920's. He lobbied for tourism in his home state extensively, and the hotel carries his name today for that dedication. The magnificent Tudor-styled architecture of the building is complemented by the extensive collection of western and Sioux Indian artifacts that fill its interior. The hotel was completed in 1928.

On a bitter, but brilliant January day in 1988, Chuck Park ventured out to capture the BN's yearly bout with winter on the Dakota prairie. A BN GP-20 and a leased EMD GP38-2 are bracketed between a wedge plow and a Jordan spreader on their trip between Madison and Wentworth.

Another view by Chuck Park, although this view in Sioux Falls lacks the action of the battle with the drifts; Winter 1988.

During early 1988, the power-short DM&E leased units from the Dakota and Iowa. D&I units 19 and 20 are switching an Aberdeen industry in the company of DM&E SD-10 556 in this photo by Jeff Hendricks.

C&NW Extra #4150 East out of Sioux Falls has reached the BN crossing just across the border at Manley, Minnesota in this view by Kevin Ryan on March 5, 1988. The train is bound for Worthington, Minnesota, and the North Western main line to the Twin Cities.

On the main line through Aberdeen, one is likely to encounter a variety of BN locomotives, plus a few from other railroads in pool service. A Union Pacific SD40-2 showed up in March 1988, and a BN cabless B30-7A belches smoke in an early April view. (Both photos, Jeff Hendricks)

Soo Line SD40-A 6409 leads two BN SD40-2's out of Aberdeen with a coal train bound for the Wisconsin Power and Light Generating Station at Columbia, Wisconsin. Number 6409 was originally Illinois Central Gulf #6022. (Jeff Hendricks photo)

GP-7 #4187 and partner back a cut of cars into the John Morrell Packing Plant in Sioux Falls in April 1988. A variety of by-products were shipped out of the plant in 40 foot box cars. (Chuck Park photo)

A BN train waits to get across the crossing with the DM&E at Huron in 1988. The gate is normally positioned against the BN, as the DM&E fields the most trains. (Steve Friezen photo)

A proud crew and well wishers join in a group photo to celebrate the Dakota Southern's first train to Kadoka on July 22, 1988. The line from Kadoka east to Chamberlain had been without service since the Milwaukee's last train on March 31, 1980. (Greg Bunce photo)

These days, the windmill has only the cattle to water on the High Plains. A North Western GP-35 leads a 98-car northbound PRBFA(Proviso Yard/Chicago to Belle Fourche) near Hermosa. The PRBFA and counterpart BFPRA were the longest freight train runs on the North Western system at the time.

A northbound PRBFA was given a railfans' dream lashup by the C&NW's Chadron roundhouse hostlers on September 12, 1988 as GP-30 #815 leads another GP-30, three GP-35's, and an ex-Rock Island GP-7 north near Whitewood.(Doug Morgan photo)

A crew is at work to rebuild the trackage in the ex-BN yards in Deadwood in the summer of 1988. The rebirth of the Deadwood Central Railroad, a privately financed venture, brought the sound of steam back to the northern Black Hills in the fall of 1988.

Photographer Chuck Park caught C&NW crew member Leon Zea "winding the clock" to reset the signals manually at Great Bear crossing east of Sioux Falls on November 5, 1988.

As the North Western pulled out of Sioux Falls in late 1988, Chuck Park recorded several views of the last trains. On November 22, the last regular crew posed on the front deck of GP-7 #4108 - from left to right are Joe Supalla-fireman, Walt Elvin-conductor, Leon Zea-brakeman, John McChesney-brakeman, and Leon Golden-engineer

In the two vertical views, a North Western GP leads a cut of cement hoppers, while on December 8th, a temporary C&NW crew uses BN power to switch West Sioux Falls one more time. Both views are from the 12th Street bridge.

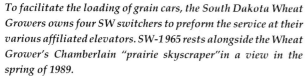

To facilitate the loading of grain cars, the South Dakota Wheat Growers owns four SW switchers to preform the service at their various affiliated elevators. SW-1 965 rests alongside the Wheat Grower's Chamberlain "prairie skyscraper" in a view in the spring of 1989.

GP-35 #848 leads a northbound PRBFA past the nearly abandoned Main Street of St. Onge on January 18, 1989.

A BN unit is sandwiched between two leased GP-38's on a run down from Mitchell to Yankton on March 9, 1989. The signboard of Napa action is barely visible in front of the BN diesel. (Chuck Park photo)

I like to call this photo "A Man and His Locomotive". On July 3, 1989, Senator Larry Pressler was honored for his help in getting the DM&E off the ground. Ex-Milwaukee Road SD-10 #550 was the first locomotive to be named on the railroad, carrying the name of the state's senior Senator. After posing for a few photos in front of the unit, the Senator was presented a certificate by DM&E President Pete McIntyre. Note in the cab window of the 550, as Huron Trainmaster Gerry Delahoy carries on the logistics and operations of the railroad during the ceremony.

A westbound DM&E "Black Hills Express" heads up the Bad River Valley in June 1989. The local historical societies have placed a number of the informational signs in the area of the Bad River to mark such trails and points of interest.

Another man, and his locomotive. Alex Huff, President of the Dakota Southern, proudly poses in front of "Centennial" SD-9 #506 at Kimball in July 1989. The unit was decorated in the colorful scheme to celebrate the state's centennial.

Dakota Southern Engineer Greg Bunce shot an eastbound DS train as it passed the abandoned stock pens at Belvidere in September 1989.

Power from both new railroads in Sioux Falls is represented in this photo on April 27, 1989. On the right, a yet to be repainted Central Vermont Railway switcher rests by the sanding tower, soon to be painted into maroon for its new owner Ellis and Eastern. Number 291 on the left is owned by the Minnesota Valley Railroad, whose subsidiary Buffalo Ridge Railroad operates the ex-C&NW trackage east of Sioux Falls to Agate, Minnesota. The E&E operates the ex-C&NW line from the yards of Sioux Falls west to Ellis. (Chuck Park photo)

One of the author's favorite places to photograph is south of Edgemont on the BN's busy main line through the southwestern part of the state. Here, a set of BN's leased Oakway SD-60's lead two BN GE's on a southbound unit coal train.

Steve Friezen caught an empty coal train on the BN's main near Garretson in the summer of 1989.

A BN grain train winds down the Garretson-Sioux Falls line near Corson in December 1989. (Mike Mancuso photo)

A BN freight pulls past the Buffalo Ridge Railroad(ex-CNW) crossing just across the border at Manley, Minnesota in December 1989. The BN's #2823 wears the railroad's new visibility scheme, created to prevent grade crossing accidents. (Mike Mancuso photo)

A unique switcher preforms the duties at the Benson-Quinn grain terminal at Corson. The Baldwin switcher is one of a few left in active service in the U.S.

Another privately owned elevator switcher, this time in the capital city of Pierre.

DM&E #550, the Larry Pressler, leads four other diesels and 108 cars west through Vayland in March 1990. Many of the original wooden elevators have met their fate, as these are about to.

If all roads lead to the famous Wall Drug, then at least one railroad does too! DM&E SD-10 #551 wears a Wall Drug sticker in Rapid City.

A lashup of Dakota and Iowa power awaits a call to duty at the quarry in Dell Rapids, March 1990.

A BN crew prepares for a trip south from Mitchell to Sioux City in March 1990. The ex-Milwaukee station and yards are nearly vacant, and the present BN operations can hardly compare to the activity of twenty years before. Even a decade before, the last orange and black was treading over the lines for the final trips.

209

Action on the Soo Line branch to Veblen on March 20, 1990. Grain is still the primary commodity on most of the branches in the state. (Steve Friezen photo)

Dakota Southern Engineer Greg Bunce(the one with the cigar) and agent "Chessie" discuss the day's work.

North Western GP-40 #5526 and three trailing units have cut off a southbound train at Buffalo Gap to make a pickup. The first railhead in the Black Hills area now sees a train but once a week.

211

A great deal of credit for this book must go to Professor Leonard Tripp of Sioux Falls. Leonard came to Sioux Falls after the Second World War, and began a collection of railroad photos and data. The son of an interurban trolley carman in New York state, he had an early interest and appreciation of the steel wheel to steel rail relationship. He also became involved in model railroading and historical pursuits in Sioux Falls. Probably his favorite project over the years has been the restoration of the South Dakota Central/Great Northern's Rutland depot, now a part of the permanent display at the W. H. Lyon Fairgrounds in Sioux Falls. The remaining photos in the chapter are examples of railroading's history that remain, or are preserved in the Land of Infinite Variety -South Dakota.

Joint C&NW/CB&Q station at Hot Springs; now the city's Chamber of Commerce.

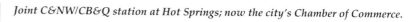

Ex-SDC/GN depot from Wentworth; On display at Pioneer Village near Madison.

Ex-Illinois Central station in Sioux Falls; currently used as offices.

Ex-Milwaukee depot at Vivian; used for storage on site.

Ex-C&NW depot at DeSmet; currently City/County museum.

Ex-M&StL/C&NW station at Watertown; preserved as museum on site.

Ex-Milwaukee depot in Yankton; currently used for offices.

Ex-C&NW depot from Blunt-Redfield line; on display at 1880 Town near Murdo.

216

Crouch Line/CB&Q promotion posters; ex-Crouch Line(RCBH&W) office at Rapid City.

Branch Mint locomotive "Natalie" from Galena; on display at Crazy Horse Memorial.

Ex-Union Pacific DD40X; on display on Dakota Southern Railway at Chamberlain.

Ex-Milwaukee FP-7 at Sioux Falls in the early 1970's (inset); on display at 1880 Town near Murdo.

Northern Hills Railway Society members Nick Heinen and Gerald Frame hike along ex-CB&Q Spearfish line in 1989.

Ex-Deadwood Central mining spur(road) and current open pit gold mining near Lead,1989.

Ex-Milwaukee turntable at Mitchell, 1990.

Ex -Milwaukee depot and freight station at Rapid City, 1990. Currently the depot is Remington's Restaurant and the freight station is vacant and for sale.

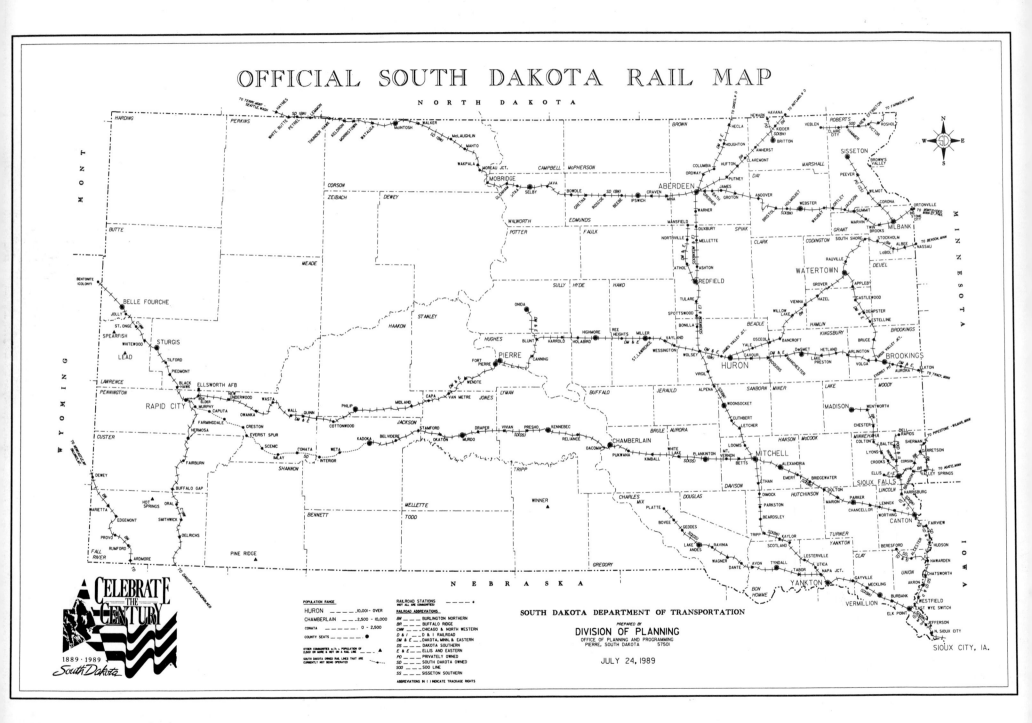

OFFICIAL SOUTH DAKOTA RAIL MAP

NORTH DAKOTA

SOUTH DAKOTA DEPARTMENT OF TRANSPORTATION

PREPARED BY

DIVISION OF PLANNING

OFFICE OF PLANNING AND PROGRAMMING
PIERRE, SOUTH DAKOTA   57501

JULY 24, 1989

SIOUX CITY, IA.

CELEBRATE THE CENTURY
1889 · 1989
South Dakota

POPULATION RANGE

HURON _____ 10,001 - OVER
CHAMBERLAIN _____ 2,500 - 10,000
CONATA _____ 0 - 2,500
COUNTY SEATS ____ ●

RAILROAD STATIONS
(NOT ALL ARE COMMUNITIES) ------- ●

RAILROAD ABBREVIATIONS

BN ____ BURLINGTON NORTHERN
BR ____ BUFFALO RIDGE
CNW ___ CHICAGO & NORTH WESTERN
D & I __ D & I RAILROAD
DM & E _ DAKOTA, MINN. & EASTERN
DS ____ DAKOTA SOUTHERN
E & E __ ELLIS AND EASTERN
PO ____ PRIVATELY OWNED
SD ____ SOUTH DAKOTA OWNED
SOO ___ SOO LINE
SS ____ SISSETON SOUTHERN

OTHER COMMUNITIES WITH A POPULATION OF
2,500 OR MORE & NOT ON A RAIL LINE ____ ▲

SOUTH DAKOTA OWNED RAIL LINES THAT ARE
CURRENTLY NOT BEING OPERATED _____

ABBREVIATIONS IN ( ) INDICATE TRACKAGE RIGHTS

C&NW's PRBFA (Chicago-Belle Fourche, SD) near Whitewood - 1988 (photo by Doug Morgan)

"Over the river" for Burlington Northern at Garretson - 1989 (photo by Kevin Ryan)

The Dakota, Minnesota & Eastern's "City of Huron" - 1990 (photo by Rick Mills)

Dakota & Iowa charges out of Sioux Falls - 1989 (photo by Kevin Ryan)

"Centennial" Grain Train on Dakota Southern at Pukwana - 1990 (photo by Rick Mills)

Black Hills Central 0-6-0 near Hill City - 1987 (photo by Rick Mills)

Outlook from an Oakway SD-60 on BN main near Edgemont - 1988 (photo by Rick Mills)

Coal train on the main near Aberdeen - 1982 (photo by Jeff Hendricks)

Shades of DM&E around the turntable at Huron - 1989 (photo by Rick Mills)

Soo Line turn at Milbank - 1988 (photo by Rick Mills)

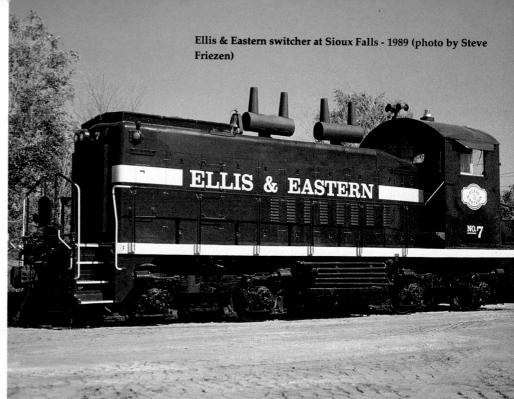

Ellis & Eastern switcher at Sioux Falls - 1989 (photo by Steve Friezen)

Buffalo Ridge Railroad grain train near Brandon - 1989 (photo by Kevin Ryan)

Sisseton-Milbank Railroad locomotive at Milbank - 1989 (photo by Rick Mills)

C&NW's "Krittenbrink & Company" at Hermosa - 1990. Left to right are Tedd Broberg, Ken Krittenbrink, and Bob Sharp. (photo by Rick Mills)

Chamberlain's "skyscraper" and railroad - 1989 (photo by Rick Mills)

"A Brakeman with a Bonnet" - Edgemont, 1987 (photo by Bob Larson)

The return of the Deadwood Central - Greg (Doc) Mason at the throttle (photo by Dan Simpson)

DM&E heads into the sunset at St. Lawrence - 1989 (photo by Rick Mills)

RECOMMENDED READING AND SELECTED BIBLIOGRAPHY

The Age of the Mad Dragons, Douglas Waitley

Burlington Route - A History of the Burlington Lines, Richard C. Overton

Chicago and North Western Steam Power, C.T. Knudsen

Chicago and North Western Power, Patrick C. Dorin

The Country Railroad Station in America, H. Roger Grant and Charles W. Bohi

Dakota Panorama - A History of Dakota Territory, Dakota Territory Centennial Commission

Diesel Locomotive Rosters, Charles W. McDonald

The Great Northern Railway - A History, Center For Western Studies

A High Line Scrapbook - The Burlington's Branch to Deadwood, Greg J. Walters and Rick W. Mills

Lines West - A Pictorial History of the Great Northern Railway, Charles R. Wood

Making the Grade - A Century of Black Hills Railroading, Rick W. Mills

The Milwaukee Road East, Patrick C. Dorin

Milwaukee Road Remembered, Jim Scribbins

The Milwaukee Road West, Charles and Dorothy Wood

North Western Rails - A Pictorial Essay of the C&NW's Western Divisions 1868-1988, Rick W. Mills

Pioneer Railroad - The Story of the Chicago and North Western System, Robert Casey and W.A.S. Douglas

Railplan South Dakota 1978-1981, 1983, 1986, 1989 - SD Department of Transportation

Railroads of the Black Hills, Mildred Fielder

Steam Locomotives of the Burlington Route, Bernard Corbin and William F. Kerka

MAGAZINES
CTC BOARD (recent and current railroad operations and histories)
Mainline Modeller (a complete listing of railroad historical societies)
RAILFAN & RAILROAD (a wide variety of historical and current railroading)
TRAINS (historical and current railroading articles)
TRAINS ILLUSTRATED (quarterly magazine devoted to high quality railroad photos)

LINE MILEAGES AND DATES OF BEGINNING OPERATIONS FOR THE MAXIMUM RAILROAD SYSTEM IN THE STATE OF SOUTH DAKOTA

Chicago and North Western	Year	Mileage	Milwaukee Road	Year	Mileage
Marshall, Minn. - Gary	1872	1.00*	Sioux City - Vermillion	1872	28.19*
Gary - Watertown	1873	34.48*	Vermillion - Yankton	1873	26.20
Minnesota Border - Sioux Falls	1878	16.20	Beloit, Iowa - Elk Point	1878	
Sioux Falls - Salem	1879	39.60	Beloit, Iowa - Sioux Falls	1879 >	33.61*
Tracy, Minn. - Volga	1879	24.61*	State Line near Canton - Marion	1879	38.47
Volga - Pierre	1880	184.50	Marion - Running Water	1879	62.85
Sioux Valley Jct. - Watertown	1880	43.83	Big Stone - Webster	1880	57.12
Watertown - Clark	1881	31.10	Pipestone - Madison	1880	37.30*
Huron - Ordway	1881	87.10	Marion - Chamberlain	1880	111.30
Clark - Redfield	1882	40.00	Mitchell - Aberdeen	1881	128.31
Hawarden, Iowa - Iroquois	1882	125.49*	Webster - Aberdeen	1881	49.90
Ordway - Columbia	1883	5.70	Madison - Woonsocket	1881	59.90
Centerville - Yankton	1884	28.46	Egan - Sioux Falls	1881	34.20
Chadron, Neb. - Buffalo Gap	1885	37.55*	Yankton - Scotland Jct.	1882	25.50
Redfield - Faulkton	1886	32.50	Aberdeen - Ellendale, ND	1882	32.72*
Buffalo Gap - Rapid City	1886	48.14	Milbank - Wilmot	1882	17.00
Columbia - Oakes, N.D.	1886	24.87*	Aberdeen - Ipswich	1883	26.50
Doland - Verdon	1886	24.38	Ortonville, Minn. - Fargo N.D.	1884	1.20*
Faulkton - Gettysburg	1887	42.65	Scotland Jct. - Mitchell	1886	47.80
Verdon - Groton	1887	14.46	Ipswich - Bowdle	1886	30.52
Salem - Mitchell	1887	32.40	Tripp - Armour	1886	20.47
Rapid City - Whitewood	1887	36.43	Andover - Brampton, N.D.	1886	38.71*
Whitewood - Belle Fourche	1890	21.19	Madison - Bristol	1887	103.02
Whitewood - Deadwood	1890	9.13	Roscoe - Eureka	1887	26.39
Buffalo Gap - Hot Springs	1890	14.12	Roscoe - Orient	1887	40.99
Belle Fourche - Aladdin, Wyo.	1899	11.90*	Wilmot - Sisseton	1893	20.10
Minn. State Line - Astoria	1900	5.80	Napa - Platte	1900	82.00
Norfolk, Neb. - Bonesteel	1902	9.63*	Bowdle - Evarts	1900	40.65
Ft. Pierre - Philip	1906	76.00	Eureka - Linton, N.D.	1902	14.05*
Rapid City - Wasta	1906	45.00	Woonsocket - Wessington Springs	1903	15.58
Philip - Wasta	1907	44.48	Armour - Stickney	1905	20.67
Pierre - Ft. Pierre	1907	1.82	Chamberlain - Murdo	1906	75.78
Bonesteel - Dallas	1907	30.45	Madison - Colton	1906	19.12
Blunt - Gettysburg	1910	39.55	Glenham - Missouri River	1906	11.65
Belle Fourche - Newell	1910	23.52	Murdo - Rapid City	1907	143.47
Dallas - Colome	1910	10.51	Colton - Renner	1907	13.96
Colome - Winner	1911	10.99	Missouri River - White Butte	1907	91.86*
Braden - Beyond Vale	1927	12.13	Trail City - Faith	1910	106.61
Jolly - Jolly Dump	1927	3.74	Moreau Jct. - Isabel	1910	59.40
Winner - Wood	1929	33.71	McLaughlin - New England, N.D.	1910	8.53*
Belle Fourche - Bentonite, Wyoming	1948	13.50			

Burlington Northern	Year	Mileage
Benson, Minn. - Watertown	1887	44.25*
Watertown - Huron	1888	69.84"
Alliance, Neb. Marietta	1889	35.65*
Pipestone, Minn. - Sioux Falls	1888	24.31*
Rutland, N.D. - Aberdeen	1889	55.00*
Marietta - Newcastle, Wyo.	1889	13.02*
Englewood - Deadwood	1890	8.00 (1)
Edgemont - Hill City	1890	59.86
Hill City - Deadwood	1891	46.54
Minnekahta - Hot Springs	1891	12.43
Garretson - Manly, Minn.	1891	10.08
Englewood - Spearfish	1893	31.91
Sioux Falls - Yankton	1893	58.34 (2)
Hill City - Keystone	1900	9.50
Sioux Falls - Colton	1904	20.00
Colton - Rutland	1905	22.00
Rutland - Watertown	1907	60.80

Minneapolis & St. Louis	Year	Mileage
Madison, Minn. - Watertown	1884	40.70
Watertown - Leola	1906	114.13
Conde - LeBeau	1907	115.47
Leola - Long Lake	1929	19.02

Rapid City, Black Hills & Western	Year	Mileage
Rapid City - Dark Canyon (Scott's Mills)	1893	8.00 (4)
Dark Canyon - Mystic	1906	26.00

Forest City & Sioux City	Year	Mileage
Forest City - Gettysburg	1890	19.00

Soo Line	Year	Mileage
Ashley, N.D.- Pollock	1901	33.56
Fairmount, N.D.- Veblen	1913	35.00
Veblen- Grenville	1914	39.25

Fremont, Elkhorn & Missouri Valley	Year	Mileage
Deadwood - Ruby Basin	1891	11.78 (6)
Portland Jct. -End of Track	1891	2.40 (6)
Mine Branches -Ruby Basin	1891	2.55 (6)
Mine Branches -Portland Jct.	1891	1.62 (6)
Gayville - Lead	1902	2.92 (4)

Illinois Central (Gulf)	Year	Mileage
Hills, Minn.- Sioux Falls	1887	14.95

Black Hills and Fort Pierre (7)	Year	Mileage
Spur near Lead	1881	0.90 (4)
Lead - near Bucks	1882	15.00 (6)
Near Bucks - Mowatt (North Line)	1890	5.00 (6)
Mowatt - Piedmont (North Line)	1891	16.57 (6)
Spur near Lead	1892	1.61 (4)
Bucks - Este	1898	13.88 (6)
Piedmont - Stage Barn	1902	2.79 (6)
Este - Merritt	1907	4.36 (6)
Este - Stage Barn	1910	10.84 (6)

Chicago, Rock Island & Pacific	Year	Mileage
Pipestone, Minn. - Watertown	1884	71.85*
Iowa State Line- Sioux Falls	1886	10.91

Deadwood Central (7)	Year	Mileage
Deadwood Englewood	1889	8.00 (1)
P1uma - Lead	1889	1.17 (6)
extension of above	1889	0.14 (6)
Kirk - Whitetail Switch	1891	1.82 (6)
Whitetail Switch - up Nevada Gulch	1891	2.44 (6)
extension from Whitetail Switch	1891	0.97 (6)
Frantail Switch - Welcome	1891	1.56 (6)
Whitetail Switch - Carthage	1893	0.70 (6)
Nevada Gulch extension	1895	0.34 (6)
Whitetai1 Creek Ext.	1895	0.87 (6)
extension of above	1898	0.03 (6)
Galena Jct. - Galena	1902	6.95 (6)
extension near Lead	1902	0.09 (6)
Mine extensions - Ruby Basin	1902	0.60 (6)

* Includes mileage for only that part of the line located within South Dakota.
(1) The first construction of this line was by the Deadwood Central in 1889 from Deadwood to Lead via Pluma. In 1890 the Grand Island & Wyoming Central purchased the line from Englewood to Deadwood, the Deadwood Central reserving the rights to lay a third rail. The third rail was laid from Deadwood to Kirk in 1891 and from Kirk to Englewood about 1905.
(2) Line shared with Chicago & North Western from Volin to Yankton.
(3) This railroad was referred to by many names, some of which were: Dakota, Western & Missouri River; Dakota, Wyoming & Missouri River; Missouri River & North Western; Dakota & Wyoming; Black Hills & Wyoming.
(4) A 3rd rail was added to existing line to permit the operation of both standard and narrow gauge equipment.
(5) The Fremont, Elkhorn & Missouri Valley Railroad was purchased by the Chicago & North Western in 1903. Additional lines built by the F.E.&M.V. are found listed under the Chicago & North Western heading.
(6) Narrow gauge rail line.
(7) The Black Hills & Ft. Pierre Railroad and the Deadwood Central Railroad were both under management of the Burlington & Missouri River Railroad by the year 1902 and later (1904) the Chicago, Burlington & Quincy Railroad Company.

Abandonments

Milwaukee Road	Year Abandoned	Total Mileage
Evarts Jct. to Evarts	1909	5.30
Springfield to Running Water	1930	6.71
Madison to 2 mi. S. of Chester	1936	13.50
S. of Huntimer to Near Colton	1936	2.80
Scotland to Tyndall	1936	11.20
Menno to Scotland	1938	8.90
Renner to Wentworth	1941	24.48
Kingsburg to Springfield	1965	5.31
Tyndall to Kingsburg	1971	6.40
Tripp to Stickney	1972	40.84
Madison to Woonsocket	1972	55.00
Garden City to Bryant	1974	25.99
Roscoe to Orient	1977	41.00
Marion Jct. to Menno	1978	21.50
Trail City to Faith	1979	106.50
Woonsocket to Wessington Springs	1979	15.20
Bristol to Garden City	1979	28.80
Moreau Jct. to Isabel	1979	56.50
Jackson, MN to Egan	1979	12.00
Andover to Brampton, ND	1980	38.60 (1)
Roscoe to Linton, ND	1980	40.70 (2)
Aberdeen to Edgeley, ND	1980	31.80
Ortonville, MN to Fargo, ND	1980	1.30
Madison to Bryant	1980	47.30
Napa to Platte	1980	82.90
Mitchell to Rapid City	1980	286.00 (4)
East Wye Switch to Mitchell	1980	116.50 (3)
East Wye Switch to Canton	1980	15.30 (3)
Canton to Mitchell	1980	78.10 (3)
Sioux Falls to Sioux Falls Jct.	1980	32.30 (5)
Egan to Madison	1980	26.00 (6)
Mitchell to Wolsey	1980	54.60 (3)
Wolsey to Aberdeen	1980	74.00 (3)
Mason City, IA to Canton, SD	1980	3.00
Sioux City to East Wye Switch	1980	14.70 (3)
Canton to Sioux Falls	1980	20.80 (3)
Ortonville to Terry, Montana	1982	299.10 (3)
Milbank to Sisseton	1982	37.10 (3)
McLaughlin to New England	1982	9.70

(3) Service reinstated under different ownership
(4) 66.6 miles restored under SD ownership.
(5) 19.5 miles owned by SD and operated by D & I Railroad.
(6) 7.4 miles restored through BN ownership

Chicago and North Western	Year Abandoned	Total Mileage
Belle Fourche to Wyoming State Line	1926	11.90
Deadwood to Lead	1928	4.37
Yankton to Mission Hill	1935	5.24
Hot Springs to Buffalo Gap	1939	14.12
Watertown Jct. to Gary	1955	33.29
Belle Fourche to Newell	1966	23.26
near Nisland to Vale	1966	12.11
Revillo to Strandburg	1968	10.50
Stratford to Leola	1968	42.70
Strandburg to Watertown	1969	22.30
Doland to Frankfort	1969	9.50
Winner to Wood	1969	33.70
Volin to Wakonda	1969	6.88
Whitewood to Deadwood	1970	9.01
Minnesota border to Astoria	1970	6.80
Doland to Groton	1970	38.60
Redfield to Gettysburg	1970	74.10
Centerville to Wakonda	1971	11.00
Minnesota border to Revillo	1971	7.90
Watertown to Stratford	1977	71.40
Doland to Clark	1977	18.70
Winner to Norfolk, Nebraska	1978	63.20
Wren, Iowa to Iroquois	1978	125.50
Jolly to Jolly Dump	1979	3.70
James Valley Jct. to Redfield	1979	33.80
Gary, SD to Tracy, MN	1980	1.00
Ellis to Mitchell	1980	65.20
Redfield to Frankfort	1980	9.70
Watertown to Clark	1981	29.50
Agate, MN to Ellis	1988	22.60 (1)

(1) 10 miles restored under different ownership (4.8 by SD ownership & 5.2 under private ownership)
(2) 14.8 mi. restored under BN ownership.

(1) Operation of line assumed in early 1989 by the Ellis and Eastern, and the Buffalo Ridge Railroad companies.

Burlington Northern	Year Abandoned	Total Mileage
Bucks to Calcite (North Line) (BH&FP)	1910	15.57
Pluma to Lead (Trolley Line) (Deadwood Cent)	1924	2.25
Galena to Galena Jct. (Deadwood Cent)	1927	6.85
Englewood to Calcite (BH&FP)	1930	41.86
Spearfish to Trojan (GI&WC)	1934	25.62
Mission Hill to Volin	1935	5.34
2 mi. S. of Chester to 1 mi. S. of Huntimer	1935	3.10
Englewood to Trojan (GI&WC)	1943	6.43
Hayti to Watertown	1972	16.15
Yankton to MP 4.1	1976	4.10
Minnekahta to Hot Springs	1977	11.90
Wentworth to Hayti	1980	49.20
Yankton to Irene	1981	17.10
Hill City to Keystone	1981	8.80
Sioux Falls to Irene	1981	41.00
Custer to Deadwood	1983	65.70
Kirk to Lead	1983	3.40
Zeeland, ND to Eureka	1985	14.80
Edgemont to Custer	1986	41.60

Chicago Rock Island & Pacific	Year Abandoned	Total Mileage
Clear Lake to Watertown	1953	24.12
Minnesota border to Clear Lake	1967	47.73
Iowa border to Sioux Falls	1972	10.91

Soo Line		
Veblen to Grenville	1971	41.65
Ashley, ND to Pollock	1987	32.80

Illinois Central (Gulf)		
Sioux Falls to Cherokee, IA	1980	14.90

Forest City & Sioux City	Year Abandoned	Total Mileage
Forest City to Gettysburg	1911	19.00

Minneapolis & St. Louis		
LeBeau to Akaska	1924	12.70
Conde to Akaska	1940	102.80
Leola to Long Lake	1940	19.02

Rapid City, Black Hills & Western		
Rapid City to Mystic	1947	34.00

Fremont, Elkhorn & Missouri Valley

All narrow gauge track was abandoned prior to 1930 under ownership of the Chicago & North Western   21.27

Black Hills & Fort Pierre

Additional abandonments totalling 57.44 miles are listed under the heading of Burlington Northern. All abandonments of Black Hills & Fort Pierre lines occurred under the management of Burlington Northern's predecessors prior to 1930.   13.51

Deadwood Central

Additional abandonments totalling 9.10 miles are listed under the heading of Burlington Northern. All abandonments of Deadwood Central lines occurred under the management of Burlington Northern's predecessors prior to 1930.   16.58

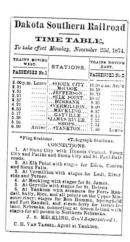

Dakota Southern Railroad

TIME TABLE,

To take effect Monday, November 23d, 1874.

TRAINS MOVING WEST.	STATIONS.	TRAINS MOVING EAST.
PASSENGER No.1		PASSENGER No.2
2.00 p.m. Leave	*SIOUX CITY	11.20 a.m. Arr've
2.31	McCOOK	10.59
3.51	JEFFERSON	10.59
3.37	*ELK POINT	10.67
3.57	BURBANK	9.33
4.21	†VERMILLION	9.09
4.53	MECKLING	8.37
5.17	GAYVILLE	8.11
5.38	*JAMES RIVER	7.52
5.56	SHOPS	7.34
6.00 Arrive	†YANKTON	7.30 Leave

*Flag Stations. †Telegraph Stations.

CONNECTIONS.

1. At Sioux City with Illinois Central, Sioux City and Pacific and Sioux City and St. Paul Railroads.
2. At Elk Point with stages for Eden, Canton and Sioux Falls.
3. At Vermillion with stages for Lodi, River side and Turner.
4. At Meckling with stages for St. James.
5. At Gayville with stages for St. Helena.
6. At Yankton with steamers for Forts Randall, Sully, Rice, and all points on the Upper Missouri river; stages for Bon Homme, Springfield and Fort Randall, and steam ferry for Green Island, Nebraska, connecting at Green Island with stages for all points in Northern Nebraska.

J. S. MECKLING, Gen'l Superintend't.

C. H. VAN TASSEL, Agent at Yankton.

The
Chicago
Milwaukee
& St. Paul
Railway

THE
CHICAGO
MILWAUKEE
AND ST. PAUL
RAILWAY

Passenger Train Schedules

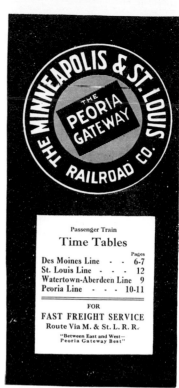

THE MINNEAPOLIS & ST. LOUIS RAILROAD CO.

THE PEORIA GATEWAY

Passenger Train

Time Tables

	Pages
Des Moines Line	6-7
St. Louis Line	12
Watertown-Aberdeen Line	9
Peoria Line	10-11

FOR
FAST FREIGHT SERVICE
Route Via M. & St. L. R. R.

"Between East and West—
Peoria Gateway Best"

JULY-AUGUST, 1928

Burlington Route

TIME TABLES

EVERY WHERE WEST

Rapid City, Black Hills

and

Western Railroad

TIME TABLE
No. 134

EFFECTIVE AT 12:01 A. M.
MOUNTAIN STANDARD TIME
SUNDAY, JUNE 23, 1946

DESTROY ALL TIME TABLES OF PREVIOUS DATES

This Time Table is for the exclusive use and guidance of all employees concerned, who must carry in addition the book of rules of the operating department. Chicago Burlington & Quincy book of rules governs all R. C. B. H. & W. R. R. employees.

GREAT NORTHERN RAILWAY

TIME TABLES

ROUTE OF THE
Air Conditioned
EMPIRE BUILDER

GLACIER NATIONAL PARK

APRIL 24, 1960

CHICAGO AND NORTH WESTERN RAILWAY

Route of the FAMOUS
"400" Streamliners

Chicago, Rock Island & Pacific Railroad

Rock Island

TIME TABLE
DES MOINES DIVISION
No. 7

EFFECTIVE AT 12:01 A.M.

SUNDAY JULY 30, 1967

STANDARD TIME
CENTRAL TIME—GOODLAND AND EAST
MOUNTAIN TIME—GOODLAND AND WEST

W. C. HOENIG Superintendent	G. H. VOSS Asst. Gen. Mgr.
W. F. THOMPSON Senior Asst. Gen. Mgr.	J. B. BUFFALO General Manager

This Time Table for the exclusive use
and guidance of employees

Dakota Division

Where Safety and Service are a Tradition

Printed in U.S.A.

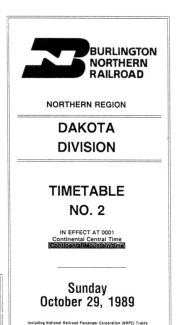

BURLINGTON NORTHERN RAILROAD

NORTHERN REGION

DAKOTA DIVISION

TIMETABLE
NO. 2

IN EFFECT AT 0001
Continental Central Time
Continental Mountain Time

**Sunday
October 29, 1989**

Including National Railroad Passenger Corporation (NRPC) Trains

Region Vice President W. W. FRANCIS	Division General Manager H. D. ROBINSON

Vice President Service Design
W. A. HATTON

Illinois Central Gulf Railroad

i

NORTHERN DIVISION

TIMETABLE NO.

1

EFFECTIVE 12:01 AM
Sunday, October 31, 1982

Superseding
Chicago Division Timetable
No. 20
Dated April 25, 1982
Iowa Division Timetable
No. 10
Dated December 27, 1981
Illinois Division Timetable
No. 11
Dated April 25, 1982
St. Louis—Missouri Division Timetable
No. 7
Dated October 25, 1981

FOR THE GOVERNMENT OF EMPLOYEES ONLY

I. B. HALL, Vice-President and Chief Transportation Officer
R. K. OSTERDOCK, Asst. Vice-President—Transportation
G. G. HESTER, General Superintendent—Transportation
J. E. MOSS, Superintendent—Transportation

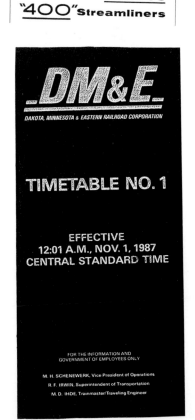

DM&E
DAKOTA, MINNESOTA & EASTERN RAILROAD CORPORATION

TIMETABLE NO. 1

**EFFECTIVE
12:01 A.M., NOV. 1, 1987
CENTRAL STANDARD TIME**

FOR THE INFORMATION AND
GOVERNMENT OF EMPLOYEES ONLY

M. H. SCHENEWERK, Vice President of Operations
R. F. IRWIN, Superintendent of Transportation
M. D. IHDE, Trainmaster/Traveling Engineer

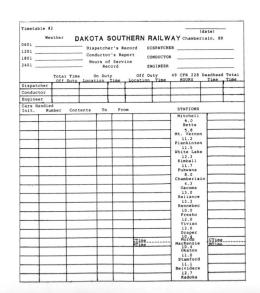

Timetable #2

DAKOTA SOUTHERN RAILWAY

(date) Chamberlain, SD

Weather

0601		Dispatcher's Record	DISPATCHER
1201		Conductor's Report	CONDUCTOR
1801		Hours of Service	
2401		Record	ENGINEER

	Total Time Off Duty	On Duty Location Time	Off Duty Location Time	49 CFR 228 HOURS	Deadhead Time	Total Time
Dispatcher						
Conductor						
Engineer						

Cars Handled Init.	Number	Contents	To	From	STATIONS		
					Mitchell		
					6.0 Betts		
					5.0 Mt. Vernon		
					11.2 Plankinton		
					11.5 White Lake		
					12.3 Kimball		
					11.7 Pukwana		
					8.0 Chamberlain		
					4.3 Oacoma		
					13.0 Reliance		
					13.2 Kennebec		
					10.0 Presho		
					12.0 Vivian		
					13.0 Draper		
					10.8 Murdo		
					10.4 MacKenzie		
					11.0 Okaton		
					11.1 Stamford		
					12.7 Belvidere		
					Kadoka		

SOO

SYSTEM TIMETABLE
NO. 6

**EFFECTIVE
0001 CONTINENTAL CENTRAL TIME
0101 CONTINENTAL EASTERN TIME

SUNDAY, OCTOBER 29, 1989**

For the government and
information of employees only.

As we conclude this look at the railroads and railroaders that have served South Dakota, one more story must be told. Pictured on the left side of the Warren-Lamb Lumber Company's narrow-gauge steamer is Charlie (Furman) Smith of Fairburn. Smith worked for the logging railroad that ran from Fairburn into Custer State Park from 1919 until the end of operations in 1927. The wreckage in the photo is from a derailment in which Furman narrowly escaped with his life. The derailment occured when the normally-dry Dry Creek was the sight of a flash flood which weakened the railroad's trestle in June 1920. He then worked for the Warren-Lamb Railroad west of Rapid City for a time. After that he returned to ranching on the family's homestead west of Fairburn, within sight of the Chicago & North Western's standard-gauge line from Rapid City to Chadron, Nebraska. He still lives in the Fairburn community, and still has a love for his work on the railroad, as well as railroads and their history in general. Furman, at 93 years of age, proudly poses with a model steamer that was given to him.

It is the intent of the author to honor all of these individuals that took pride in their service on the various lines in the state. For their contributions to the development of the state as we know it, a thank you is extended.